AI

FOR BEGINNERS 2026

Learn ChatGPT, Gemini, Claude, Generative AI & Automation Without Coding- A Practical Guide for Real-World Applications

AJAYA NAYAK

AI for Beginners 2026

This eBook is intended for educational and informational purposes only. While every effort has been made to ensure the accuracy and reliability of the information presented, the author makes no guarantees regarding completeness, accuracy, or applicability. The reader is responsible for how they choose to use the information provided.

The technologies, tools, and examples discussed in this book are subject to continuous change due to the rapidly evolving nature of Artificial Intelligence. The author does not assume responsibility for any outcomes resulting from the use of this information.

Author: Ajaya Nayak

Edition: First Edition, 2026

ISBN: (To be assigned)

Disclaimer: This book does not provide legal, financial, or professional advice. Readers are encouraged to seek appropriate professional guidance where necessary.

CONTENTS

This book is dedicated to all learners, beginners, and curious minds who are taking their first step into the world of Artificial Intelligence.

ABOUT THE AUTHOR

Ajaya Kumar Nayak is an experienced technology leader, educator, and passionate advocate for making Artificial Intelligence accessible to everyone—regardless of background, age, or technical expertise.

With a Master's degree in Computer Science and Engineering and an Executive Senior Management Program from the Indian Institute of Management (IIM) Visakhapatnam, Ajaya combines strong technical depth with strategic leadership. Over the years, he has earned multiple certifications across wireless technologies, cloud computing, Artificial Intelligence, networking, and project management (PMP), reflecting his continuous commitment to learning and innovation.

Ajaya brings over 22 years of professional experience spanning Telecommunications (PSTN, 2G, 3G, 4G, and 5G), Cloud Computing, Kubernetes, Containers, Artificial Intelligence, Consulting, and Education. Throughout his career, he has collaborated with leading global organizations such as AT&T, T-Mobile, Meta, Amazon, Nokia, Ericsson, Cisco, Dish Network,

Exfo, Capgemini, NEC, and Fujitsu. For more than a decade, he has been actively supporting major clients in the United States, contributing to large-scale technology transformations and strategic initiatives.

Beyond his professional achievements, Ajaya is deeply committed to education and mentorship. He has guided thousands of individuals and supported numerous organizations in understanding and adopting emerging technologies, particularly in the fields of telecommunications, cloud and AI. His ability to simplify complex concepts and translate them into practical knowledge has made him a trusted mentor and coach.

A strong believer that **AI literacy is one of the most essential skills of the 21st century**, Ajaya authored "*AI for Beginners 2026*" with a clear mission: to bridge the gap between complex AI technologies and real-world understanding. His goal is to empower learners, professionals, and curious minds to confidently navigate the evolving world of Artificial Intelligence.

Outside of his professional work, Ajaya enjoys reading, mentoring students and colleagues, exploring new technologies, and staying updated with the latest advancements in AI. He also finds joy in music, singing, watching movies, playing cricket, and gardening—bringing balance and creativity into his everyday life.

Through his work, Ajaya continues to inspire others to learn, adapt, and grow in an AI-driven world.

Connect with the Author:

- 💼 **LinkedIn:** [linkedin.com/in/ajaya kumar nayak]
- 📧 **Email:** [nayak.ajaya@gmail.com]

CHAPTER BREKDOWN

PART 1: FOUNDATIONS — UNDERSTANDING AI BASICS

"Before you can master AI, you must understand what it truly is"

Chapter 1: What Is Artificial Intelligence?

- What Artificial Intelligence really means
- What Generative AI is
- Common myths and realities about AI
- How AI thinks vs. how humans think
- Types of AI: Narrow AI, General AI, and Super AI
- Why AI matters more than ever in 2025 and beyond

Chapter 2: The AI Ecosystem and Key Concepts Explained Simply

- Machine Learning, Deep Learning, and Neural Networks demystified

- Natural Language Processing (NLP), how machines understand language
- Computer Vision, how machines see the world
- What is GPT (Generative Pre-trained Transformer)
- Generative AI the Technology Changing Everything
- Agentic AI the Next Evolution of Intelligent Systems
- Key terminology every reader must know

Chapter 3: Generative AI-Large Language Models (LLMs), Tokenization & Vector Embeddings

- What is Generative AI?
- What is an LLM?
- User Request → Model Flow (High-Level)
- What is Tokenization?
- Embeddings
- Vector Databases
- What is RAG?

Chapter 4: The Big Players Shaping AI Today

- OpenAI and the rise of GPT
- Google DeepMind and Gemini

- Anthropic and the story of Claude
- Meta, Microsoft, Amazon, and others
- How these companies compete and collaborate
- Which AI is right for which purpose?

PART 2: MEET THE AI GIANTS: GPT, CLAUDE & GEMINI

"Know your tools before you use them"

Chapter 5: GPT: The Pioneer That Changed Everything

- The story of ChatGPT and why it shocked the world
- How GPT models work (simply explained)
- GPT-4o, Gpt-5 and the latest capabilities
- Best use cases: writing, coding, research, creativity
- Strengths and limitations of GPT
- Hands-on: Your first GPT prompt walkthrough

Chapter 6: Claude: The Thoughtful AI

- Who is Anthropic and why they built Claude differently
- Claude's core philosophy: safety, honesty, and helpfulness

- Which AI wins at safety and reliability?
- How to choose the right AI for your specific needs
- The smart approach: using all three strategically

PART 3: PROMPTING MASTERY: TALK TO AI LIKE A PRO

"The quality of your output depends entirely on the quality of your input"

Chapter 9: The Art and Science of Prompting

- What is prompt engineering and why it matters
- The anatomy of a perfect prompt
- Setting the stage, defining the task, specifying rules
- Zero-shot, one-shot, and few-shot prompting explained
- Common prompting mistakes beginners make

Chapter 10: Advanced Prompting Techniques

- Chain-of-thought prompting
- Role-based prompting giving AI a persona
- Iterative prompting refining outputs step by step

- Prompt templates for common professional tasks
- Building your personal prompt library

Chapter 11 Prompting GPT, Claude & Gemini Differently

- Why the same prompt gives different results across models
- Tailoring prompts for GPT's strengths
- Tailoring prompts for Claude's strengths
- Tailoring prompts for Gemini's strengths
- Real-world prompt examples with actual outputs compared

PART 4: AI IN ACTION: REAL WORLD APPLICATIONS

"AI is only as valuable as what you do with it"

Chapter 12: AI for Personal Productivity

- Managing emails, calendars, and tasks with AI
- AI-powered note-taking and summarization
- Learning faster with AI as your tutor
- AI tools for everyday life

Chapter 13: AI for Business and Professionals

- AI in marketing: content, SEO, social media
- AI in finance: analysis, forecasting, reporting

PART 1

FOUNDATIONS- UNDERSTANDING AI BASICS

"Before you can master AI, you must understand what it truly is"

CHAPTER 1

WHAT IS ARTIFICIAL INTELLIGENCE?

INTRODUCTION

Artificial Intelligence, commonly known as AI, is one of the most transformative technologies of our time. From smartphones and online shopping recommendations to self-driving cars and virtual assistants, AI is becoming an essential part of our everyday lives.

Yet for many beginners, AI can feel confusing, technical, or even intimidating. News headlines often describe AI as either a revolutionary miracle or a dangerous threat to humanity. This creates unnecessary fear and misunderstanding.

Artificial Intelligence is not magic, and it is not science fiction. It is a technology designed to help machines perform tasks that normally require human intelligence. AI systems can learn patterns, analyze information, solve problems, and assist people in making better decisions.

This book is designed to help beginners understand AI in a simple, practical, and student-friendly way. You do not need a programming background or advanced technical knowledge to understand the concepts discussed here. All you need is curiosity and a willingness to learn.

By the end of this chapter, you will understand:

- What Artificial Intelligence really means
- What Generative AI is
- Common myths and realities about AI
- How AI differs from human thinking
- Different types of AI systems
- Why AI is becoming more important than ever in 2025 and beyond

Let us begin our journey into the fascinating world of Artificial Intelligence.

WHAT IS ARTIFICIAL INTELLIGENCE (AI)?

Artificial Intelligence refers to computer systems or software that are designed to perform tasks that usually require human intelligence.

These tasks may include:

- Understanding language
- Recognizing images or speech
- Solving problems
- Learning from data
- Making predictions
- Automating decisions

In simple words, AI allows machines to "learn" from information and improve their performance over time.

Today, AI is already part of daily life for millions of people around the world. Many people use AI regularly without even realizing it.

For example:

- Voice assistants like Siri and Alexa use AI to understand spoken language.
- Netflix and YouTube use AI to recommend movies and videos.
- Banks use AI systems to detect fraudulent transactions.
- Online shopping platforms use AI to suggest products based on customer interests.
- Navigation apps like Google Maps use AI to predict traffic conditions and suggest faster routes.

AI is not limited to large technology companies. It is now being used in healthcare, education, agriculture, finance, transportation, entertainment, and many other industries.

As technology continues to improve, AI will become even more integrated into our personal and professional lives.

WHAT IS GENERATIVE AI?

Generative AI is a type of artificial intelligence that can **create new content** such as text, images, audio, video, or code based on patterns it has learned from existing data.

Unlike traditional AI systems that mainly analyze or classify information, Generative AI can produce original content based on patterns it has learned from large amounts of data.

You can think of Generative AI as a creative digital assistant.

For example, Generative AI tools can:

- Write essays and articles
- Create presentations
- Generate artwork and illustrations
- Compose music
- Build computer programs
- Answer questions conversationally
- Help students learn difficult subjects

Some popular examples of Generative AI tools include:

- ChatGPT
- Gemini
- Claude
- DALL·E
- GitHub Copilot
- DeepSeek

One of the main reasons Generative AI has become so popular is its accessibility. Earlier technologies often required specialized technical skills. Today, anyone who can type a question or describe an idea can use AI tools effectively.

This has opened new opportunities for students, professionals, entrepreneurs, teachers, and content creators around the world.

COMMON MYTHS AND REALITIES ABOUT AI

There are many misconceptions about Artificial Intelligence. Movies, social media, and sensational news headlines often create unrealistic expectations and unnecessary fear.

Understanding the difference between myths and reality is essential for developing a balanced and informed perspective.

Myth 1: AI Is a Robot

Reality: Most AI Exists as Software

When many people think about AI, they imagine humanoid robots that look and behave like humans. In reality, most AI systems today are software programs running on computers and cloud servers.

Applications like ChatGPT, Google Translate, Netflix recommendations, and voice assistants are all examples of AI software.

Although AI can be integrated into robots, the "intelligence" itself is software rather than the physical machine.

Myth 2: "AI Thinks Like Humans"

Reality: Ai Recognizes Patterns, Not Emotions

AI systems do not think, feel emotions, or possess consciousness like humans.

Instead, AI analyzes enormous amounts of data and identifies patterns. It then generates responses or predictions based on those learned patterns.

For example, when you ask ChatGPT a question, it does not "understand" the question emotionally or consciously. It predicts the most appropriate response based on the information it learned during training.

While AI can sometimes appear intelligent or human-like, its underlying process is fundamentally mathematical and statistical.

Myth 3: "AI Knows Everything"

Reality: AI only knows what it was trained on and AI can make mistakes.

AI systems are not perfect.

They only know information based on the data they were trained on. Sometimes AI tools can generate incorrect or misleading responses. This issue is commonly known as an "AI hallucination."

Therefore, users should always verify important information, especially for:

- Medical advice
- Legal information
- Financial decisions
- Academic research

- Time-sensitive topics

Critical thinking remains extremely important in the age of AI.

Myth 4: "AI will replace all human jobs"

Reality: AI will transform jobs, not simply eliminate them

History shows us that transformative technologies the printing press, electricity, the internet always change the way people worked. They eliminate some jobs, transform many others, and create entirely new categories of work that nobody anticipated.

AI is following the same pattern. Some repetitive tasks may become automated, but many new opportunities will also emerge. Human skills such as creativity, leadership, emotional intelligence, communication, and ethical judgment will continue to remain valuable.

People who learn how to work alongside AI will likely have significant advantages in the future workplace.

Myth 5: "AI is only for tech experts"

Reality: AI is becoming accessible to everyone

Modern AI tools are designed to be user-friendly.

Today, students, teachers, writers, business owners, marketers, designers, and many other professionals can use AI without advanced coding knowledge. If you can type a sentence, ask a question, or explain an idea, you can begin using AI tools effectively.

This accessibility is one of the biggest reasons AI adoptions is growing so rapidly worldwide.

A BRIEF HISTORY OF ARTIFICIAL INTELLIGENCE

The concept of Artificial Intelligence has existed for decades.

1950: Alan Turing and the Turing Test

British mathematician and computer scientist Alan Turing introduced an important question:

"Can machines think?"

He proposed the famous "Turing Test," designed to evaluate whether a machine could imitate human conversation convincingly enough to appear human.

This idea became one of the foundations of AI research.

1950s–1960s: Early AI Research

Researchers developed rule-based systems capable of solving mathematical problems and playing simple games.

During this period, scientists were highly optimistic about the future of AI.

1970s–1980s: The AI Winters

Progress in AI slowed significantly due to limited computing power and unrealistic expectations.

Funding and public interest decreased during these periods, which became known as "AI winters."

1990s–2000s: The Rise of Machine Learning

AI research shifted toward machine learning, where systems learned from data rather than relying entirely on manually written rules.

One major milestone occurred in 1997 when IBM's Deep Blue defeated world chess champion Garry Kasparov.

This demonstrated the growing capabilities of AI systems.

2010s: The Deep Learning Revolution

Advancements in computing power, graphics processing units (GPUs), and large datasets led to major breakthroughs in deep learning.

AI systems achieved remarkable success in:

- Image recognition
- Speech processing
- Language understanding
- Translation

2020s: The Era of Generative AI

Generative AI tools such as OpenAI's ChatGPT and image-generation systems like DALL·E introduced AI capabilities to millions of everyday users.

For the first time, people around the world could interact with highly advanced AI systems using simple natural language.

This marked the beginning of a new era of accessibility and innovation.

HOW AI THINKS COMPARED TO HUMANS

Although AI systems may sometimes appear intelligent, they operate very differently from humans.

Human Learning

Humans can learn from:

- Personal experiences
- Emotions
- Context
- Social interaction
- Small numbers of examples

Humans are also capable of creativity, ethical reasoning, empathy, and imagination.

AI Learning

AI systems learn by analyzing large amounts of data and identifying statistical patterns.

In most cases, AI requires thousands or even millions of examples to perform effectively.

AI can process information extremely quickly, but it lacks:

- Self-awareness
- Emotions
- Conscious understanding

TYPES OF ARTIFICIAL INTELLIGENCE

AI systems are generally divided into three categories based on capability.

1. **Narrow AI (Weak AI)**

   Narrow AI is designed to perform specific tasks.

   Examples include:

   - Voice assistants
   - Recommendation systems
   - Facial recognition
   - Spam filters
   - Navigation systems

   Most AI applications used today belong to this category.

2. **General AI (Strong AI)**

   General AI refers to a theoretical system capable of performing any intellectual task that a human can do.

   Such systems would be able to:

   - Learn across multiple domains
   - Reason independently
   - Adapt to unfamiliar situations

   At present, General AI does not yet exist.

3. **Super AI**

   Super AI refers to hypothetical systems that could surpass human intelligence in every area.

   This concept remains speculative and is often discussed in science fiction and future focused research debates. Currently, there is no Super AI system in existence.

WHY AI MATTERS MORE THAN EVER IN 2025 AND BEYOND

AI is becoming increasingly important due to several major developments.

1. **Rapid Growth of Data**

   Modern society generates enormous amounts of digital data every day.

AI helps organizations analyze this information efficiently and identify useful insights.

2. **Increased Computing Power**

   Cloud computing, GPUs, and specialized AI hardware have made advanced AI systems more accessible and affordable.

3. **Real-World Applications Across Industries**

   AI is transforming many sectors, including:

Healthcare

- Faster disease detection
- Improved diagnostics
- Drug discovery
- Personalized treatments

Education

- Personalized learning experiences
- AI tutors and study assistants
- Automated grading systems

Business

- Customer service automation
- Market analysis
- Process optimization

Climate and Agriculture

- Weather prediction
- Smart farming
- Resource optimization

AI is no longer a futuristic concept. It is a practical technology shaping industries and societies today.

CONCLUSION

Artificial Intelligence is one of the most important technological advancements of the modern era.

Although AI may sometimes seem complex, its core purpose is simple: helping machines perform intelligent tasks that can support human activities and decision-making.

In this chapter, you learned:

- The meaning of Artificial Intelligence
- The role of Generative AI
- Common myths and realities about AI
- Differences between human thinking and AI processing
- Various types of AI systems
- Why AI is becoming increasingly important worldwide

As you continue through this book, you will explore practical applications, tools, ethical considerations, and real-world examples that will help you understand how AI can be used responsibly and effectively.

The future of AI is not only for scientists or technology experts. It is for students, professionals, entrepreneurs, and lifelong learners who are willing to understand and adapt to a rapidly changing world.

Your journey into Artificial Intelligence has just begun.

CHAPTER 2

THE AI ECOSYSTEM

INTRODUCTION

Artificial Intelligence is not a single technology. Instead, it is a vast ecosystem made up of multiple technologies, concepts, tools, and techniques working together to create intelligent systems.

Every time you interact with a chatbot, receive movie recommendations, unlock your phone using facial recognition, or translate text instantly, several branches of AI are operating behind the scenes.

For beginners, the world of AI can sometimes feel overwhelming because of the many technical terms used in conversations, articles, and online tutorials. Words like *Machine Learning*, *Deep Learning*, *Neural Networks*, *Natural Language Processing*, and *Generative AI* may sound complicated at first.

However, once you understand how these technologies connect with each other, the AI landscape becomes much easier to understand.

Think of the AI ecosystem as a large digital city.

Each technology has its own role:

- Machine Learning helps systems learn from data.
- Deep Learning enables AI to recognize complex patterns.
- Natural Language Processing helps machines understand human language.
- Computer Vision allows systems to "see" and interpret images and videos.
- Generative AI creates entirely new content such as text, images, music, and code.

Together, these technologies form the foundation of modern Artificial Intelligence.

Whether you are:

- A student exploring future career opportunities,
- A professional looking to stay competitive,
- A business owner wanting to understand AI trends,
- Or simply a curious learner,

understanding the AI ecosystem is one of the best starting points for your journey.

In this chapter, we will simplify the most important AI concepts in a clear and beginner-friendly way. You will learn:

- The difference between AI, Machine Learning, and Deep Learning
- How Natural Language Processing works
- What Computer Vision is
- What is GPT (Generative Pre-trained Transformer)
- How Generative AI creates content
- Important AI terminology every beginner should know
- How all these technologies connect together

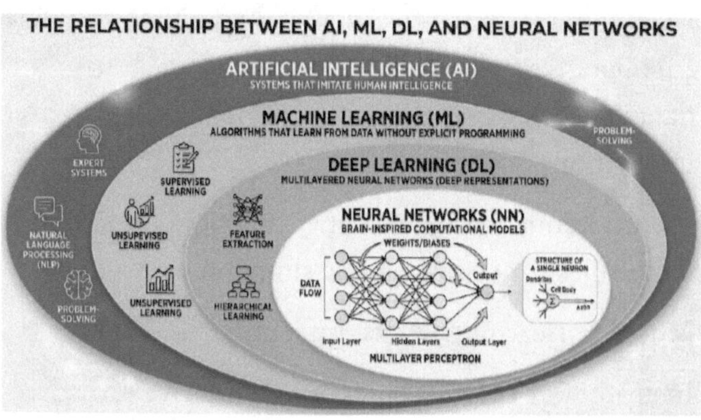

By the end of this chapter, you will have a strong foundation for understanding the modern AI world and the technologies shaping the future.

MACHINE LEARNING, DEEP LEARNING, AND NEURAL NETWORKS DEMYSTIFIED

One of the biggest reasons Artificial Intelligence feels confusing to beginners is the number of technical terms or jargons people use interchangeably.

You may often hear terms like Machine Learning, Deep Learning, Neural Networks and AI Models.

At first, these concepts may sound highly technical or intimidating. However, once broken down into simple ideas, they become much easier to understand.

Let us simplify them step by step.

What Is Machine Learning?

Machine Learning (ML) is a branch of Artificial Intelligence that enables computers to learn from data instead of being directly programmed with fixed instructions.

In traditional programming, developers manually write rules for every possible situation.

Machine Learning works differently.

Instead of giving computers every rule, we provide:

- Large amounts of data

- Examples
- Patterns

The machine then "learns" from those examples and improves over time.

A Simple Real-Life Example

Imagine teaching a child to recognize cats and dogs.

You show the child hundreds of pictures and explain:

- "This is a cat."
- "This is a dog."

Over time, the child starts identifying new pictures correctly without needing further explanation.

Machine Learning works in a very similar way.

The AI system studies data, identifies patterns, and learns how to make predictions on new information.

Common Uses of Machine Learning

Machine Learning is already being used in many applications we use every day, including:

- Netflix movie recommendations
- YouTube video suggestions
- Spam email detection
- Fraud detection in banking
- Product recommendations in online shopping

- Face recognition in smartphones

These systems continuously improve as they process more data.

What Is Deep Learning?

Deep Learning is a more advanced branch of Machine Learning.

It is inspired by the structure of the human brain and uses systems called *Neural Networks* to process information. Deep Learning becomes especially useful when dealing with Images, Videos, Speech, Natural language, Complex patterns.

While traditional Machine Learning may require humans to manually identify important features in data, Deep Learning systems can automatically discover those patterns on their own. This makes Deep Learning extremely powerful.

Understanding Neural Networks

Neural Networks are the foundation of Deep Learning. They are designed to imitate, in a simplified way, how neurons in the human brain communicate with each other.

A neural network consists of layers of connected "neurons" that process information step by step.

Think of It Like This

Imagine a team of workers in a factory:

- The first group identifies simple patterns
- The second group combines those patterns
- The final group makes a decision

For example, in facial recognition:

- One layer detects edges
- Another detects shapes
- Another identifies eyes, nose, and mouth
- The final layer recognizes a person's face

The deeper the network becomes, the more complex patterns it can understand.

This is why Deep Learning has achieved major breakthroughs in:

- Self-driving cars
- Voice assistants
- Medical imaging
- Language translation
- AI chatbots

Machine Learning vs. Deep Learning

Although the two terms are related, they are not identical.

Machine Learning

- Learns from structured data
- Often works well with smaller datasets
- Requires more human guidance
- Uses algorithms like decision trees and regression

Deep Learning

- Uses large neural networks
- Performs better with massive amounts of data
- Learns complex patterns automatically
- Excels in speech, images, and language tasks

In simple terms:

All Deep Learning is Machine Learning, but not all Machine Learning is Deep Learning.

Example: Building a Spam Email Filter

Let us understand this with a practical example.

Suppose you want to build a system that can detect spam emails.

Step 1: Collect Data

Gather thousands of emails labeled:

- Spam
- Not Spam

Step 2: Train the Model

The Machine Learning algorithm studies patterns such as:

- Suspicious words
- Repeated phrases
- Email structure
- Sender behavior

Step 3: Make Predictions

Once trained, the model can analyze new emails and predict whether they are spam.

For more advanced language understanding, Deep Learning models can analyze entire sentence structures and context more accurately. This is how modern email services protect inboxes every day.

NATURAL LANGUAGE PROCESSING (NLP): HOW MACHINES UNDERSTAND LANGUAGE

Natural Language Processing empowers machines to read, interpret, and generate human language.

Natural Language Processing, commonly called NLP, is the branch of AI that helps computers understand, interpret, and generate human language.

NLP is one of the most exciting areas of AI because it allows humans to communicate with machines naturally.

Every time you Chat with ChatGPT, Use Google Translate, speak with Alexa or Siri, Search on Google, Receive autocorrect suggestions you are interacting with NLP systems.

How NLP Works

Although NLP is highly advanced, the basic process can be simplified into a few steps.

1. **Text Processing**

   The AI cleans and organizes the text by removing unnecessary symbols, breaking sentences into smaller parts and Identifying keywords.

2. **Converting Words into Numbers**

   Computers do not understand words directly. Therefore, words are converted into mathematical representations called *embeddings*. These embeddings help AI understand relationships between words and meanings.

3. **Pattern Learning**

   The AI model studies enormous amounts of language data to identify patterns in Grammar, Meaning, Sentence structure and Context.

4. **Generating Responses**

   Finally, the system produces predictions or responses such as answering questions, translating languages, summarizing articles and detecting emotions in text.

Real-World Example: Product Review Analysis

Companies often use NLP to analyze customer reviews.

For example:

- Positive reviews may indicate customer satisfaction.
- Negative reviews may reveal product issues.

AI systems can automatically process thousands of reviews within minutes and identify customer sentiment. This helps businesses improve products and services faster.

COMPUTER VISION: HOW MACHINES SEE THE WORLD

Computer Vision is the branch of AI that enables machines to understand and interpret visual information like Images, Videos, Facial expressions, Objects and Environments.

In simple words, Computer Vision teaches machines how to "see."

Everyday Examples of Computer Vision

Computer Vision is used in:

- Self-driving cars
- Face unlocks systems on smartphones

- Medical image analysis
- Security surveillance
- Retail inventory tracking
- Social media photo tagging

Key Tasks in Computer Vision

Image Classification

Identifying what appears in an image like Cat, Dog, Car, Tree

Object Detection

Finding and locating multiple objects inside an image.

Example: A self-driving car identify Pedestrians, Traffic lights, Vehicles, Road signs, Lanes, Obstacles

Using advanced Deep Learning models called Convolutional Neural Networks (CNNs), the AI can make driving decisions in real time. This allows vehicles to respond quickly and safely to changing road conditions.

Image Segmentation

Dividing an image into meaningful sections for detailed analysis. This is especially useful in medical imaging and autonomous driving.

WHAT IS GPT (GENERATIVE PRE-TRAINED TRANSFORMER)

GPT is a highly trained language model using large amount of text, that reads your input, understands context, and predicts the best possible human like response.

- **Generative** → It can create content such as text, answers, stories, or even code.
- **Pre-trained** → It has already learned from a vast amount of data before you start using it.
- **Transformer** → A special type of AI model architecture designed to understand and process language efficiently.

GPT is built using a concept in AI known as the Transformer architecture. The Transformer uses something called attention. Attention means the model focuses on the most important words in a sentence to understand its meaning.

How GPT is Structured (Simplified)

You can think of GPT as layers of understanding:

- **Input Layer:** Takes your text (prompt)
- Multiple Transformer Layers

1. Analyze relationships between words
2. Understand context

3. Refine meaning step by step

- **Output Layer:** Generates the final response

This layered approach allows GPT to produce meaningful and coherent answers.

How Does GPT Work?

Step 1: You Give an Input (Prompt): Explain AI in simple terms by writing question in text.

Step 2: Text is Broken into Tokens: Breaks text into smaller units called tokens (words or parts of words).

Step 3: Understanding Context: Using the Transformer and attention mechanism, GPT Identifies relationships between words, understands intent and meaning.

Step 4: Predicting the Next Word: GPT generates responses **one word at a time.** It predicts based on the learned patterns "What is the most likely next word based on the context?". This process continues until a complete response is formed.

Step 5: Final Response: User receive a natural, human-like answer.

GPT works based on Language patterns, Context understanding and Probability (what comes next logically). GPT does not "think" or "understand" like a human; however, it predicts based on learned patterns.

GENERATIVE AI: THE TECHNOLOGY CHANGING EVERYTHING

Generative AI is one of the most revolutionary advancements in modern Artificial Intelligence. Unlike traditional AI systems that mainly analyze information, Generative AI can create entirely new content like Text, Images, Video, Article, Music, Content, Presentations, Documents.

Generative AI acts like a creative assistant that collaborates with humans.

Popular Examples of Generative AI

Some well-known Generative AI tools include ChatGPT, Gemini, Claude, DALL·E, Midjourney, GitHub Copilot etc....

These systems can produce human-like content within seconds.

How Generative AI Works

Generative AI models are trained using enormous datasets containing Text, Images, Audio, Code and all.

The AI learns patterns from this data and uses those patterns to generate new content.

For example:

- ChatGPT generates text responses
- DALL·E creates images from text descriptions

- AI music tools compose original music

This technology is transforming industries such as Education, Marketing, Entertainment, Software development, Content creation and many more.

AGENTIC AI: THE NEXT EVOLUTION OF INTELLIGENT SYSTEMS

What is Agentic AI?

Imagine an AI that doesn't just respond to your commands but can think, plan, decide, and act on your behalf. Agentic AI act as **independent agent.**

Agentic AI refers to artificial intelligence systems that behave like autonomous agents. These systems are capable of understanding goals, breaking them down into actionable steps, making decisions, executing tasks, and continuously learning from outcomes. Unlike traditional AI tools, such as chatbots that simply respond to prompts, Agentic AI takes initiative and works toward completing objectives.

In simple terms, traditional AI answers your questions, whereas Agentic AI solves your problems.

Simple Analogy

Imagine hiring a personal assistant. You give them a goal, and they figure out how to complete it. That is exactly what Agentic AI does digitally.

Core Components of Agentic AI

To understand how Agentic AI works, think of it as a **digital worker with a brain, memory, and tools.**

1. **Goal / Objective**

   Every agent starts with a goal.

   Example: *"Book the cheapest flight for next weekend."*

2. **Perception (Input Layer)**

   The agent gathers information from User input, APIs, Databases and Real-time data.

3. **Reasoning Engine (LLM Brain)**

   This is the thinking layer (often powered by large language models). It decides "What to do next" and "how to solve the problem".

4. **Planning Module**

   Breaks the goal into smaller steps like Search flights, Compare prices, Select best option and Book ticket.

5. **Tools / Actions Layer**

   The agent interacts with external systems like Web browser, APIs, Software tools and Automation platforms.

6. **Memory**

   Two types:

   - Short-term memory → Current task context

- Long-term memory → Past interactions and learning

7. **Feedback Loop (Learning)**

   The agent learns and improves by Evaluating results, Adjusting decisions and Learning from success/failure.

How, Agentic AI Works (Step-by-Step Flow)

The working of Agentic AI can be understood as a continuous cycle of understanding, planning, acting, and improving. It begins when a user provides a goal, such as planning a business trip. The system first interprets the request and breaks it into smaller tasks like booking flights, reserving hotels, and scheduling meetings.

Once the tasks are identified, the agent creates an execution plan that outlines the sequence of actions required. It then interacts with various tools and platforms to carry out these actions, such as searching travel websites or accessing calendar applications. After each action, the agent evaluates whether the results meet the desired criteria, such as budget or timing.

If the results are not satisfactory, the agent adjusts its approach by exploring alternatives. This cycle continues until the objective is successfully achieved, at which point the agent delivers a complete and optimized outcome, such as a finalized travel itinerary.

Let's simplify the working into a logical flow:

Step 1: Understand the Goal

User gives a task → *"Plan a business trip to New York."*

Step 2: Analyze & Break Down

Agent divides the task to Book flight, Reserve hotel and Schedule meetings.

Step 3: Plan Execution

Creates a sequence of actions: Search flights→Compare prices→Check hotel availability

Step 4: Take Action

Uses tools like Travel APIs, Booking platforms and Calendar tools

Step 5: Evaluate Results

Checks whether "The flight within budget"? and "Is the timing suitable"?

Step 6: Adjust if Needed

If something fails, try alternative flights and suggest better options

Step 7: Deliver Outcome

Itinerary booked, travel plan created and calendar updated.

Why Agentic AI Matters

Agentic AI is powerful because it reduces manual effort, enhances decision-making, and enables systems to operate continuously without human intervention. It is capable of handling complex, multi-step tasks that would otherwise require significant time and coordination.

More importantly, it represents a shift in how we interact with technology. Instead of using AI merely as a tool, we begin to work with it as a digital collaborator that actively contributes to achieving our goals.

Agentic AI vs Traditional AI

To understand Agentic AI, it is important to see how AI has evolved.

Traditional AI systems are reactive. They wait for your input and respond accordingly. For example, if you ask a chatbot a question, it provides an answer but it does not take further action unless you ask again.

Then came Generative AI, which can create content. Tools like ChatGPT can write emails, generate ideas, or even help you code. However, they still rely heavily on user prompts.

Agentic AI is the next step in this evolution. Instead of just responding or generating content, it can **take initiative.** It understands your goal, plans the steps required, executes tasks, and adjusts its approach if needed.

Think of it like this:

- Traditional AI is like a **calculator**
- Generative AI is like a **writer**
- Agentic AI is like a **personal assistant**

This shift is powerful because it changes AI from a passive tool into an active problem solver.

No-Code Agent Building

One of the most exciting aspects of Agentic AI is that you don't need programming skills to get started.

No-code platforms allow you to build workflows by connecting actions visually. For example, you can create an agent that reads emails, extracts key information, and sends responses automatically.

These platforms are designed for beginners and provide a hands-on way to understand how Agentic AI works. By experimenting with simple workflows, you can gradually build more complex systems.

Risks and Challenges

While Agentic AI is powerful, it is not without risks. One of the main challenges is over-reliance, where users depend too heavily on AI without verifying results.

Another issue is inaccuracies, sometimes referred to as hallucinations, where AI generates incorrect information. Data privacy is also a concern, especially when sensitive information is involved.

Understanding these risks is essential to using Agentic AI responsibly and effectively.

The Future of Agentic AI

The future of Agentic AI is incredibly promising. We are moving toward a world where AI agents can handle complex tasks across industries, from healthcare to finance to education.

In the future, AI agents may act as personal assistants, business operators, and even decision-makers. This will transform how work is done and create new opportunities for those who understand and adopt this technology.

The key will be collaboration between humans and AI, where each complements the other's strength.

Popular Agentic AI Tools

As Agentic AI continues to evolve, a growing ecosystem of tools is making it easier for beginners and professionals to build and use intelligent agents.

Today, several platforms allow you to interact with AI agents without needing deep technical expertise. Tools like ChatGPT (with advanced capabilities), Microsoft

Copilot, and Google Gemini are integrating agent-like behaviors by helping users complete multi-step tasks. More advanced frameworks such as AutoGPT and agent-based systems enable AI to act autonomously by planning and executing tasks.

It is important to understand the difference between **no-code, low-code, and developer-focused tools.** No-code tools are ideal for beginners and allow you to create workflows using simple interfaces. Low-code platforms require some technical understanding but offer more flexibility. Developer tools provide full control but require programming knowledge.

Choosing the right tool depends on your goal. If you want to automate daily tasks, no-code tools are sufficient. If you want to build complex systems, advanced frameworks may be required.

Real-World Use Cases of Agentic AI (with Flow)

Use Case 1: AI Personal Assistant (Daily Productivity)

Scenario: Manage your daily schedule

Flow:

- Input → "Plan my day"
- Agent checks calendar
- Prioritizes tasks
- Schedules meetings

- Sends reminders
- Adjusts based on delays

Outcome: A fully optimized day without manual effort

Use Case 2: Customer Support Automation

Scenario: Handle customer queries automatically

Flow:

- Customer raises issue
- Agent understands intent
- Searches knowledge base
- Provides solution
- If unresolved → escalates to human
- Learns from interaction

Outcome: Faster resolution, reduced workload

Use Case 3: Software Development Assistant

Scenario: Build a simple application

Flow:

- Input → "Create a login page"
- Agent plans: UI design, Backend logic
- Generates code
- Tests functionality
- Fixes errors

- Deploys application

Outcome: End-to-end development with minimal human input

Use Case 4: Business Process Automation

Scenario: Automate invoice processing

Flow:

- Receive invoice
- Extract data (AI vision + NLP)
- Validate details
- Enter into system
- Notify finance team
- Flag anomalies

Outcome: Faster operations with fewer errors

Use Case 5: E-commerce Smart Agent

Scenario: Optimize product pricing

Flow:

- Monitor competitor prices
- Analyze demand trends
- Adjust pricing automatically
- Run promotions
- Track performance
- Optimize continuously

KEY TERMINOLOGY EVERY READER MUST KNOW

To navigate the AI ecosystem confidently, you'll encounter:

- **Algorithm:** A set of rules or procedures for solving a problem.
- **Model:** The trained mathematical representation that makes predictions.
- **Training:** The process of teaching a model by feeding it data.
- **Dataset:** A collection of examples used for training or evaluation.
- **Parameter:** A value within the model that adjusts during training.
- **Inference:** Applying a trained model to new data to generate predictions.
- **Overfitting:** When a model learns the training data too closely and performs poorly on new data.
- **Loss Function:** A metric that measures how far the model's predictions are from the true values.
- **Epoch:** One complete pass through the entire training dataset.

- **Embedding:** A mathematical representation of words, images, or other data.
- **Token:** is the basic unit of text or data that a model processes to understand and generate language

CONCLUSION

The AI ecosystem is made up of many interconnected technologies working together to create intelligent systems.

In this chapter, you explored Machine Learning, Deep Learning, Neural Networks, Natural Language Processing, Computer Vision, Generative AI, Agentic AI, Essential AI terminology.

Although these concepts may initially seem complex, they become much easier once broken down into simple ideas and real-world examples. The most important thing to remember is you do not need to become a scientist or programmer overnight to understand AI. Every expert in AI started as a beginner. By learning step by step and staying curious, you can gradually build a strong understanding of the technologies shaping the future.

Keep the momentum going your journey into AI mastery has only just begun!

CHAPTER 3

GENERATIVE AI-LARGE LANGUAGE MODELS (LLMS), TOKENIZATION & VECTOR EMBEDDINGS

INTRODUCTION

Generative AI is one of the most powerful and transformative technologies of our time. It powers tools that can write content, generate code, summarize information, answer questions, and even assist in solving complex problems.

At the core of this revolution are **Large Language Models (LLMs)**, advanced AI systems designed to understand and generate human-like language.

But an important question arises: **How do these systems actually work?**

When you interact with tools like ChatGPT, Gemini, Claude, DeepSeek or Llama, the responses may feel natural and intelligent. However, behind the scenes, a fascinating process is taking place.

This process is built on two key ideas:

- Tokenization (breaking language into smaller pieces)
- Vector Embeddings (converting language into numbers that machines can understand)

Although these terms may sound technical, the concepts are simple and incredibly powerful.

In this chapter, you will learn:

- What Generative AI is and why it matters
- How text is broken down into tokens
- How meaning is represented using vectors
- How LLMs process this information
- How systems generate intelligent responses step by step
- How components like embeddings and semantic search work together

By the end of this chapter, you will have a clear understanding of how Generative AI works from input to output.

WHAT IS GENERATIVE AI?

Generative AI refers to a type of Artificial Intelligence that can create new and original content based on patterns it has learned from large datasets.

Unlike traditional AI systems that mainly analyze or classify data, Generative AI can produce completely new outputs like

- Text (ChatGPT, Gemini, Claude, DeepSeek, Perplexity, NotebookLM)
- Images (DALL·E, Imagen, Midjourney, Canva, Nano banana, Higgsfield, Heygen)
- Code (Claude Code, Copilot, ChatGPT-Codex, Cursor)
- Audio & Video (Higgsfield, Heygen, Kling, Canva)

At the core of most modern Generative AI systems is a **Large Language Model (LLM).**

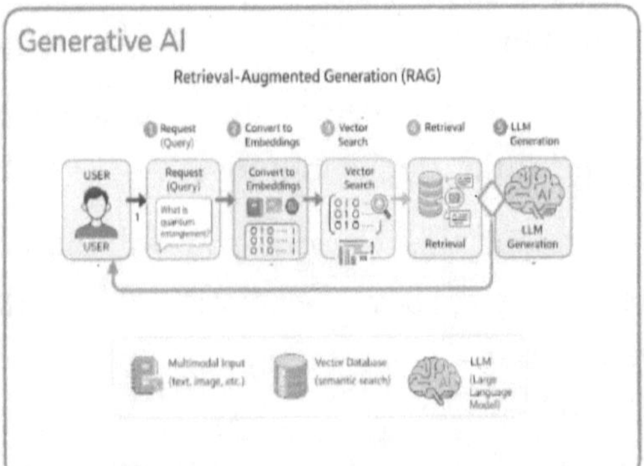

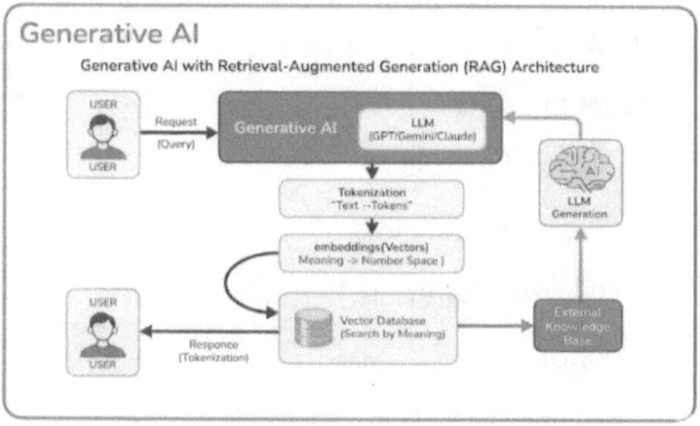

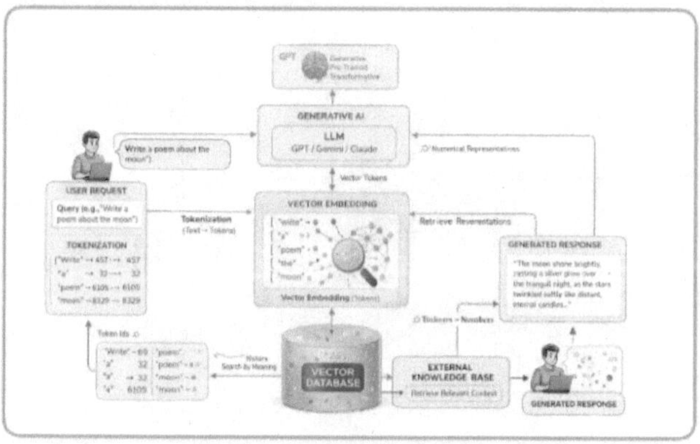

WHAT IS AN LLM (LARGE LANGUAGE MODEL)?

An LLM is a type of AI model trained on massive amounts of text data, such as Books, Articles, Websites, Conversations, Code repositories.

By learning from this data, the model understands Language patterns, Grammar and structure, Context and meaning and Relationships between words.

This allows it to generate responses that feel natural and human-like.

Examples of LLM:

- GPT (OpenAI)
- Gemini (Google)
- Claude (Anthropic)
- Grok (xAI)
- Llama (Meta)
- DeepSeek (DeepSeek)

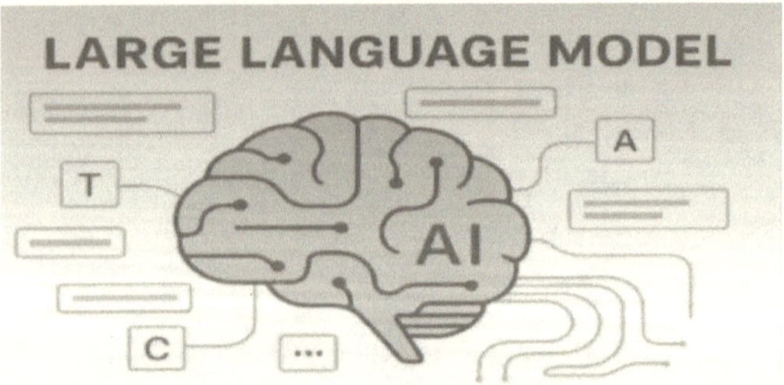

Key Idea

An LLM

does not understand language like humans. Instead, it:

- Converts text into numbers
- Learns statistical patterns
- Predicts the

- next most likely token

LLMs are **probability machines over tokens.**

USER REQUEST → MODEL FLOW (HIGH-LEVEL)

- User sends a
- query (text)
- Text is
- tokenized
- Tokens are converted into
- numerical representations
- Model processes the numbers using neural networks
- Model generates
- output tokens
- Tokens are converted back into readable text

TOKENIZATION (TEXT → TOKENS)

What is Tokenization?

Tokenization is the process of **breaking text into smaller units called tokens.**

Example:

- Input: "Write a poem about the moon"

- Tokens: ["Write", "a", "poem", "about", "the", "moon"]

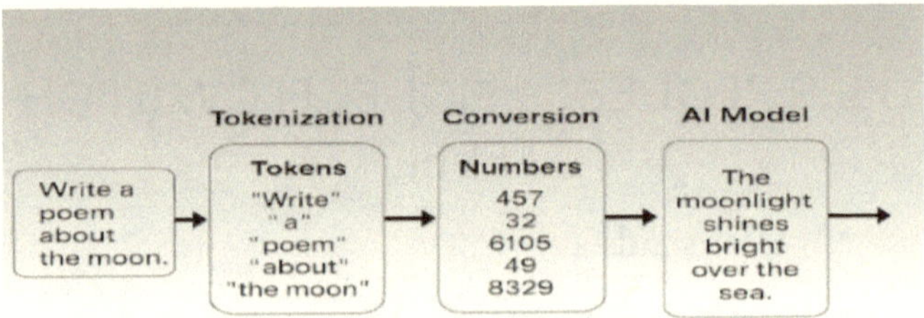

Why Tokenization?

- Neural networks
- cannot process raw text
- They work only with
- numbers

Each token maps to a **unique numeric ID.**

TOKENS → NUMBERS

After tokenization:

- "Write" → 457
- "a" → 32
- "poem" → 6105
- "moon" → 8329

These numbers are **indexes** into the model's vocabulary.

EMBEDDINGS (MEANING → VECTOR SPACE)

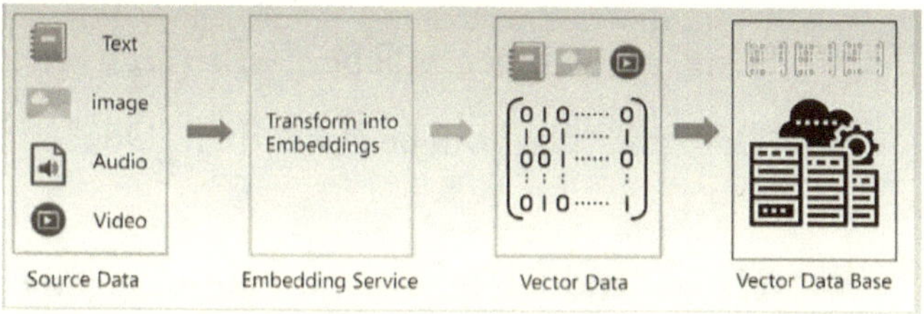

What are Embeddings?

Embeddings are numerical representations of text. They convert words, sentences, or even entire documents into a format that machines can understand.

Since computers cannot directly understand human language, they rely on numbers. Embeddings act as a bridge between human language and machine understanding.

- Text → Numbers (Vectors)
- Similar meanings stay closed.

For example, a word like *"king"* or a sentence like *"AI is transforming the world"* is converted into a list of numbers, also known as a **vector.**

These numbers may look meaningless to humans, but for machines, they carry important information about meaning and context.

Meaning is encoded as **position in multidimensional space**

For example:

- "King" and "Queen" will be close to each other
- "Dog" and "Cat" will be closer than "Dog" and "Car"
- "Happy" and "Joyful" will be grouped together

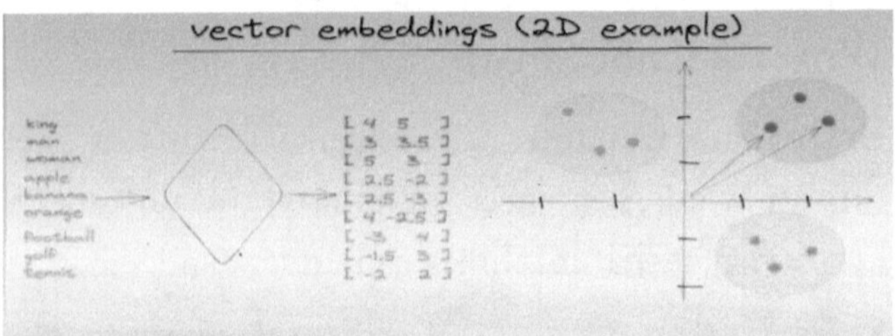

Why Embeddings Matter

Embeddings are essential because they enable AI systems to Understand context and meaning, compare different pieces of text, find similar content (semantic search), Improve recommendations and generate more accurate responses.

Without embeddings, modern AI systems would not be able to understand or generate meaningful language.

WHY SIMILAR MEANINGS STAY CLOSE

This allows AI systems to understand relationships between words, even if the exact words are different.

Examples from vector space:

- king – man + woman ≈ queen
- walk → walked
- country → capital

This happens because embeddings capture **semantic relationships.**

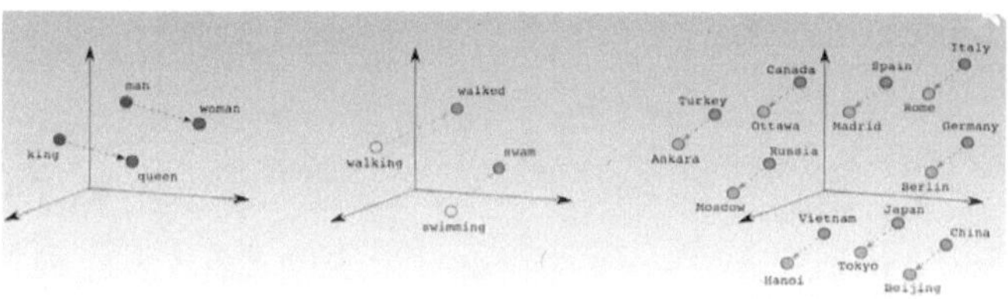

Male-Female Verb Tense Country-Capital

CLUSTERING IN VECTOR SPACE

One of the most powerful features of embeddings is that they naturally organize similar meanings into groups, known as clusters.

When words, sentences, or documents are converted into vectors, items with similar meanings are placed close to each other in the vector space. Over time, this creates clear groupings based on meaning.

How Clustering Works

Imagine a map where every word is represented as a point. Words that share similar meanings are positioned near each other, forming clusters.

For example:

Animals Cluster

- cat
- dog
- lion

Vehicles Cluster

- car
- truck
- vehicle

This allows **semantic search** instead of keyword search.

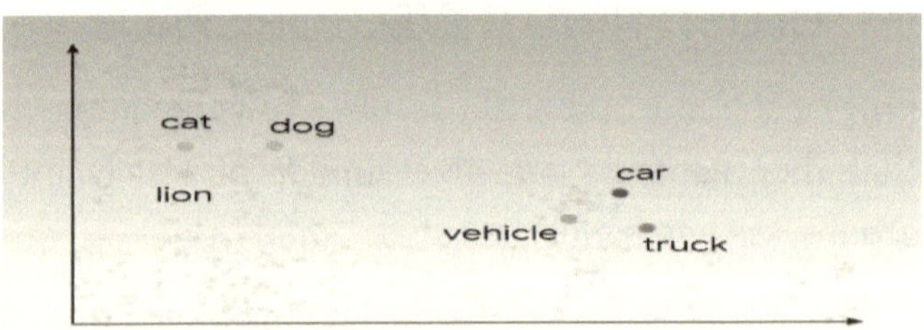

VECTOR DATABASES

What is a Vector Database?

A **Vector Database** is a specialized type of database designed to store and manage embeddings.

As you learned earlier, embeddings are numerical vectors that represent the meaning of words, sentences, or documents. A vector database stores these embeddings in an organized way and allows systems to search based on **meaning**, not just exact words.

This is what makes modern AI systems much more powerful than traditional databases.

Why Do We Need Vector Databases?

Traditional databases are excellent at storing structured data such as names, numbers, dates and exact text matches. However, they struggle when it comes to understanding meaning.

For example:

- Searching for "car" may not return results for "automobile"
- Searching for "AI tools" may miss "artificial intelligence software"

Vector databases solve this problem by enabling **semantic search**, where results are based on meaning rather than exact keywords.

Some widely used vector databases are Pinecone, Weaviate, FAISS, Milvus, Vertex AI Vector Search

HOW VECTOR SEARCH WORKS

Vector search is the process of finding the most similar embeddings based on meaning.

Here is a simple step-by-step explanation:

- **Step 1: Convert Query into an Embedding:** When a user enters a query (for example, "best cars for families"), the system converts this text into a numerical vector.
- **Step 2: Search for Similar Vectors:** The system then searches the vector database to find embeddings that are closest to the query vector.
- **Step 3: Retrieve Relevant Results:** Finally, the system returns the most relevant documents, answers, or results based on similarity.

How Similarity Is Measured

To determine how close two vectors are, AI systems use mathematical techniques such as:

- Cosine Similarity (measures how similar two vectors are in direction)
- Distance Metrics (such as Euclidean distance)

The closer the vectors, the more similar their meanings.

Real-World Example

Imagine you are searching for "Affordable electric cars". Even if the database contains documents using phrases like: "budget EV vehicles", "low-cost electric automobiles" a vector database can still retrieve them because it understands the **meaning,** not just the exact words.

RAG (RETRIEVAL-AUGMENTED GENERATION)

What is RAG?

Retrieval-Augmented Generation, commonly known as RAG, is a powerful technique that makes AI systems more accurate, reliable, and useful. In simple terms, RAG allows an AI system to:

- Search for relevant information from external sources
- Use that information to generate a better and more informed response

Instead of relying only on what it learned during training, the AI can access additional knowledge from Documents, Databases, Websites and Company knowledge bases.

This makes the response more **accurate, up-to-date, and context-aware.**

Why Do We Need RAG?

Large Language Models (LLMs) are powerful, but they have some limitations:

- They have a training cutoff (they may not know recent information)
- They can sometimes generate incorrect answers (known as hallucinations)
- They do not automatically access private or company-specific data

RAG solves these problems by combining the strengths of:

- Search systems (retrieval)
- Language models (generation)

How RAG Works (Step-by-Step)

Let us break down the RAG process into simple steps:

- **Step 1: User Query:** The user asks a question.
- **Step 2: Convert Query into Embedding:** The question is converted into a vector representation.

- **Step 3: Search Vector Database:** The system searches a vector database to find relevant information.
- **Step 4: Retrieve Context:** The most relevant documents or data are selected.
- **Step 5: Combine Query + Context:** The retrieved information is added to the original query.
- **Step 6: Generate Response:** The LLM processes both the query and the retrieved context to generate a grounded and accurate response.

Why RAG Is Important

RAG significantly improves AI performance by:

- Reducing incorrect or misleading answers
- Providing up-to-date information
- Allowing access to private or company-specific data
- Improving trust and reliability

Real-World Applications of RAG

RAG is widely used in:

- Customer support chatbots
- Enterprise knowledge systems

- Document search and analysis
- Legal and financial assistants
- Internal company tools

It is one of the most important techniques used in modern AI applications.

MULTIMODAL EMBEDDINGS

Modern AI systems are no longer limited to just text. They can now work with multiple types of data, including Text, Images, Audio, Video.

These are called **multimodal embeddings**, where all types of data are converted into a shared vector space.

Why Multimodal Embeddings Matter

Because everything is represented in the same format (vectors), AI systems can perform advanced tasks such as:

- Text → Image search (search images using text descriptions)
- Image → Text search (describe or find meaning in images)
- Cross-modal understanding (connect different types of data)

This enables more intelligent and flexible AI systems.

RESPONSE GENERATION

After retrieving relevant information, the AI generates the final response.

This process works as follows:

- The LLM predicts the next word (or token) step by step
- These tokens are combined to form meaningful text
- The final response is generated and sent to the user

Even at this stage, everything is still based on tokens and probabilities.

CONCLUSION

In this chapter, you explored the core building blocks that power modern Generative AI systems. What may initially seem like complex technology becomes much clearer when broken down into simple, connected ideas.

You learned how language is transformed into **tokens**, how meaning is captured through **embeddings**, and how similar concepts naturally form **clusters** in vector space. You also discovered how **vector databases** enable AI systems to search based on meaning rather than exact words, making interactions more intelligent and relevant.

One of the most important concepts covered was **Retrieval-Augmented Generation (RAG).** By combining external knowledge retrieval with language generation, RAG helps AI systems provide more accurate, up-to-date, and context-aware responses. This is what allows modern AI to move beyond static knowledge and interact with real-world information.

You also explored how AI is evolving beyond text through **multimodal embeddings**, enabling systems to understand and connect text, images, audio, and video within a shared space. This opens the door to more advanced and interactive applications across industries.

Finally, you saw how everything comes together in the **response generation process**, where AI predicts and constructs meaningful answers step by step using tokens.

The key takeaway from this chapter is simple:

Artificial Intelligence does not "think" like humans. Instead, it uses mathematical representations, patterns, and probability to understand and generate language.

By understanding these foundational concepts, you are no longer just a user of AI, you are someone who understands how it works behind the scenes.

In the next chapter, we will take the next step in your journey by exploring practical tools, platforms, and frameworks that you can start using to apply these concepts in real-world scenarios.

Your journey into mastering AI continues.

CHAPTER 4

THE BIG PLAYERS SHAPING AI TODAY

INTRODUCTION

In the world of Artificial Intelligence, all the leading companies and research organizations driving innovation at an extraordinary pace.

From systems that can write and code to technologies that can see, speak, and make decisions, AI is transforming how we live and work. Behind these advancements are organizations that are not only competing but also collaborating to push the boundaries of what machines can achieve.

For beginners, this landscape may seem complex. There are many companies, tools, and technologies to understand. However, once you learn who the key players are and how they operate, the AI ecosystem becomes much clearer and easier to navigate.

In this chapter, you will:

- Discover the major companies leading AI innovation
- Understand how they compete and collaborate
- Learn how to choose the right AI tools for your needs
- Explore the core technologies behind modern AI systems

Let us begin by exploring the organizations shaping the future of Artificial Intelligence.

OPENAI AND THE RISE OF GPT

OpenAI is one of the most influential organizations in the AI space. Its mission is to ensure that Artificial General Intelligence benefits all of humanity.

Its flagship models, GPT (Generative Pre-trained Transformers), have demonstrated remarkable capabilities in understanding and generating human-like language.

Key Strengths:

- **Versatility:** GPT models can write essays, generate code, answer questions, and even assist in learning complex subjects.

- **Accessibility:** OpenAI provides APIs that allow developers, startups, and businesses to easily integrate AI into their applications.
- **Focus on Safety:** The company invests in ethical AI development and works to reduce misuse.

Real-World Example

A small e-learning company used GPT to build a personalized tutoring system that adapts to each student's learning pace greatly improving engagement and outcomes.

GOOGLE DEEPMIND AND GEMINI

Google DeepMind combines advanced research with large-scale computing infrastructure, making it one of the most powerful AI organizations in the world.

Key Achievements:

- **AlphaGo:** The first AI system to defeat a world champion in the game of Go
- **Energy Optimization:** Reduced data center energy usage using AI
- **Gemini:** A next-generation model capable of understanding text, images, and context together

Real-World Impact:

A biotech startup used DeepMind's protein prediction models to accelerate drug discovery, saving significant time and resources.

ANTHROPIC AND CLAUDE

Anthropic is a relatively new but highly respected AI company focused on building safe and reliable AI systems.

Key Features:

- **Claude Model:** Designed to provide helpful and transparent responses
- **Safety First Approach:** Strong focus on reducing harmful outputs
- **Developer-Friendly Tools:** APIs with built-in safeguards

Real-World Impact:

Think of Claude as a knowledgeable and careful friend who happens to have expertise in almost everything like writing, law, medicine, business, tech. Unlike a quick Google search, Claude doesn't just hand you a list of links. It sits down with you, understands your actual question, and gives you a thoughtful, honest answer. And crucially it tells you when it doesn't know, rather than pretending it does.

META, MICROSOFT, AMAZON, AND OTHER TITANS

Beyond the pure AI labs, technology giants leverage AI to fortify their core businesses:

- **Meta:** Powers newsfeed ranking, moderate harmful content, and experiments with AI-driven VR and AR experiences in the Metaverse.
- **Microsoft:** Partners with OpenAI for Azure AI services, embeds language models in Office tools, and builds enterprise solutions through GitHub Copilot.
- **Amazon:** Uses AI in every corner from product recommendations and warehouse robotics to AWS SageMaker, which lets developers build and deploy custom models at scale.

IBM's Watson focuses on healthcare and finance.

NVIDIA accelerates AI hardware with GPUs and software libraries, and startups around the world push niche innovations.

Key takeaway: Even if you never use a "big name" API directly, these companies shape the tools, platforms, and standards that ripple through the entire AI ecosystem.

COMPETITION AND COLLABORATION: THE AI ECOSYSTEM

Although these companies compete, they also collaborate in many ways:

- **Open-Source vs Proprietary Models:** Platforms like Hugging Face make AI accessible, while companies continue to develop advanced private models
- **Industry Collaboration:** Organizations work together to establish ethical standards and safety guidelines
- **Shared Research:** Many companies publish research that benefits the global AI community

This balance between competition and collaboration accelerates innovation and makes AI more accessible to everyone.

WHICH AI IS RIGHT FOR WHICH PURPOSE?

Selecting the best AI solution depends on your goals, resources, and tolerance for complexity:

- **Rapid prototyping and general tasks:** Use hosted APIs (OpenAI, Anthropic, Azure OpenAI, Amazon Bedrock). No infrastructure to manage.

- Customization and data privacy: Fine-tune open-source models on your own servers or private cloud (Hugging Face, Meta's LLaMA, local deployment with NVIDIA containers).
- **Cost-sensitive at scale:** Balance inference costs against performance. For simple text tasks, smaller models may suffice; for multimodal research, invest in high-capacity offerings like Gemini.
- **Industry-specific needs:** Healthcare and finance often demand specialized compliance; look for vendors offering domain-trained models and robust audit logs.
- **Motivational note:** Start with a clear problem statement, experiment iteratively, and don't be afraid to pivot when a new model emerges.

CONCLUSION

The modern AI landscape is shaped by a combination of visionary companies and powerful technologies.

Organizations like OpenAI, Google DeepMind, and Anthropic are leading innovation, while major technology companies continue to integrate AI into everyday products.

At the same time, foundational technologies such as Machine Learning, Natural Language Processing,

Computer Vision, and Generative AI are driving these advancements.

The most important takeaway is this: **AI is not just for large organizations; it is for everyone who is willing to learn and explore.**

As a beginner, you now have a clear understanding of:

- Who is building AI
- How AI technologies work
- How to choose the right tools

As you continue your journey, remember that learning AI is not about mastering everything at once. It is about building knowledge step by step.

Stay curious, keep experimenting, and embrace the opportunities that AI offers.

The future of AI is not something to observe, it is something you can actively be a part of.

PART 2

MEET THE AI GIANTS-GPT, CLAUDE & GEMINI

"Know your tools before you use them"

CHAPTER 5

GPT THE PIONEER THAT CHANGED EVERYTHING

THE STORY OF CHATGPT AND WHY IT SHOCKED THE WORLD

In November 2022, something remarkable happened. A simple chat interface quietly entered the world and within days, it changed how millions of people perceived Artificial Intelligence. That tool was **ChatGPT.**

Students began using it to generate essay ideas. Developers discovered they could write and debug code faster. Writers and marketers found a creative partner that could brainstorm endlessly. For many people, it was their very first real interaction with AI.

What made ChatGPT so powerful was not just its intelligence but its **ability to communicate naturally.**

It could answer questions, explain concepts, write stories, and even adapt its tone depending on the user. This moment marked a major shift.

Before ChatGPT, AI often felt distant something limited to research labs or specialized industries. But now, AI was accessible to everyone.

For the first time, anyone with an internet connection could interact with a system trained on vast amounts of human knowledge.

HOW GPT MODELS WORK (SIMPLY EXPLAINED)

At its core, GPT (Generative Pre-trained Transformer) is a **text prediction system.** It works by learning patterns in language. During training, the model is exposed to massive amounts of data including Books, Articles, Websites, Code, images, videos etc.

From this data, GPT learns how words are structured, how sentences flow, how ideas connect.

A Simple Analogy

Imagine GPT as a smart assistant completing a sentence.

If you say: "The sun rises in the…"

GPT predicts the most likely next word: "east"

It does this not by understanding the world like a human, but by recognizing patterns it has learned. Behind the scenes, GPT uses a powerful architecture called a **transformer**, which allows it to understand context, focus on important words, generate meaningful responses.

Each response is built step by step, predicting one word (or token) at a time.

GPT-4O AND ITS CAPABILITIES

Modern GPT models have evolved far beyond text. GPT-4o (where "o" stands for "omni") is a **multimodal system**, meaning it can work with text, images, audio and video.

What This Means for You

- You can upload an image and ask for analysis
- You can provide audio and get transcriptions
- You can combine multiple inputs for richer interactions

It also offers improved reasoning, better accuracy and larger context understanding

This allows GPT-4o to handle more complex tasks, from analyzing documents to assisting in creative and technical workflows.

GPT-5 AND ITS LATEST CAPABILITIES

GPT-5 represents a major step forward in artificial intelligence, combining advanced reasoning, multimodal understanding, and task execution into a unified, highly capable system. Unlike earlier models, it can dynamically adjust between quick responses and deeper, multi-step problem solving, making it effective for everything from simple queries to complex analysis and coding. It supports text, images, and real-world context, enabling more natural and interactive use, while also offering improved accuracy and reduced errors. With emerging "agent-like" abilities, GPT-5 can plan, use tools, and complete workflows rather than just respond to prompts, marking a shift from AI as a passive assistant to an active productivity partner for learning, work, and decision-making.

BEST USE CASES: WRITING, CODING, RESEARCH, CREATIVITY

GPT's versatility shines in everyday tasks:

- **Writing:** Draft emails, blog posts, social media copy, or even novels.
- **Example:** A marketer asks, "Write a 150-word LinkedIn post announcing our new sustainability initiative." GPT supplies a polished draft in seconds.

- **Coding:** Generate snippets, refactor functions, or debug errors.
- **Example:** A beginner developer pastes a Python error trace and asks, "Why am I getting this Index Error?" GPT pinpoints the issue and offers a corrected loop.
- **Research:** Summarize articles, compare studies, extract key insights.
- **Example:** A graduate student pastes an abstract and asks for bullet points of methodology and findings, saving hours of reading.
- **Creativity:** Brainstorm ideas, Create stories, scripts, and content, Plan events, lessons, or campaigns
- **Example:** Planning a themed party? GPT can propose menus, décor ideas, and a music playlist all aligned with your chosen theme.

Each of these use cases begins with a clear prompt. The more specific you are desired length, tone, format the better the model responds. But even open-ended prompts often yield surprisingly useful results.

STRENGTHS AND LIMITATIONS OF GPT

Strengths:

- **Speed:** Instant responses replace hours of manual research or drafting.
- **Fluency:** Natural language output reads like it came from a skilled writer.
- **Adaptability:** Handles countless domains technical, creative, academic.
- Accessibility: Low barrier to entry just type your request and go.

Limitations:

- **Hallucinations:** GPT can invent facts or references that sound plausible but are false. Always verify critical information.
- **Biases:** Trained on human-generated text, the model can reflect societal biases or stereotypes. Guard against insensitive outputs.
- **Context window:** Even GPT-4o has finite memory; very long documents may be truncated or lose coherence.
- **No genuine understanding:** GPT models predict patterns; they don't "understand" concepts like a human expert. For complex reasoning, human oversight remains crucial.

By recognizing these limits, you can harness GPT safely using it as a fast assistant, not an infallible oracle.

HANDS-ON: YOUR FIRST GPT PROMPT WALKTHROUGH

Let's run through a simple example: planning a one-day workshop on "Introduction to AI."

1. **Define your goal.**

   "I need a workshop outline for beginners covering AI basics."

2. **Choose a clear prompt.**

   "Create a 3-hour workshop outline with four sessions: history of AI, how AI works, hands-on demo, ethics and future. Include time allocations and activity ideas."

3. **Set the tone.**

   Add: "Use a motivational, friendly tone suitable for complete beginners."

4. **Send the prompt.**

   Paste into ChatGPT or GPT-4o or GPT-5. Wait a few seconds.

5. **Review and refine.**

   Suppose it suggests 45-minute sessions but you prefer 40. Ask, "Please adjust each session to 40 minutes and add a 10-minute Q&A slot at the end."

6. **Iterate until it's right.**

   You might request more interactive activities or a slide deck template. GPT adapts on the fly.

By following these steps' goal, prompt, tone, review, refine—you'll master prompt-engineering best practices.

CONCLUSION

GPT has transformed Artificial Intelligence from a complex research concept into a practical tool used by millions every day.

In this chapter, you learned:

- How ChatGPT changed global perception of AI
- How GPT models work
- The capabilities of modern models like GPT-4o and GPT-5
- Real-world applications across industries
- Strengths and limitations of GPT systems

The most important takeaway is this: **GPT is not just a tool, it is a powerful assistant that can enhance your productivity, creativity, and learning.**

However, it is most effective when used thoughtfully, with awareness of its limitations.

The future of AI is not just about technology, it is about how you choose to use it

CHAPTER 6

CLAUDE THE THOUGHTFUL AI

INTRODUCTION

In the rapidly evolving world of Artificial Intelligence, new innovations frequently reshape our expectations. Among these, **Claude** stands out not just for its capabilities, but for its thoughtful and responsible design. Developed by Anthropic, Claude represents a new approach to AI one that prioritizes safety, honesty, and usefulness alongside performance.

Whether you are a beginner exploring AI for the first time, a student looking for deeper understanding, or a professional aiming to improve productivity, Claude is designed to help you work more effectively and responsibly.

WHO IS ANTHROPIC AND WHY THEY BUILT CLAUDE DIFFERENTLY

Anthropic was founded in 2021 by a group of researchers and engineers including veterans from OpenAI decided the AI community needed a new approach. They saw great promise in large language models but worried about unchecked behaviors: hallucinations, biased outputs, or even malicious misuse. Anthropic set out to prove that AI can be both capable and carefully aligned with safety and human values.

Anthropic set out to address these challenges by designing AI systems that are not only powerful but also responsible.

Key Principles Behind Anthropic:

- **Research-Driven Approach:** Focus on understanding AI behavior at scale
- **Constitutional AI:** A system guided by high-level principles like safety, honesty, and helpfulness
- **Transparency:** Openly sharing research findings, including limitations and failures

This approach led to the creation of Claude an AI assistant designed to balance intelligence with responsibility.

CLAUDE'S CORE PHILOSOPHY: SAFETY, HONESTY, AND HELPFULNESS

At the heart of Claude lies a simple three-pillar creed. By emphasizing these values, Claude offers interactions you can trust:

1. **Safety:** Claude is designed to avoid generating harmful or inappropriate content. If a request involves risky or unsafe actions, Claude will either decline or provide safer alternatives.
2. **Honesty:** Claude aims to provide accurate information and openly acknowledges uncertainty. Instead of generating misleading answers, it may suggest verifying information when needed.
3. **Helpfulness:** Claude focuses on delivering responses that are useful and relevant. It adapts its tone and depth depending on your needs, whether you want a quick summary or a detailed explanation.

CLAUDE'S UNIQUE STRENGTHS: LONG CONTEXT, NUANCED REASONING

What sets Claude apart from many other AI assistants? Two standout capabilities:

Massive Context Window: Claude can process and remember tens of thousands of words in a single conversation. You could feed it an entire research report, a legal contract, or a novel draft and it will track themes, facts, and user corrections across that span.

Example: Paste a 20-page PDF and ask, "What are the three biggest risks the author identifies?" Claude scours the entire document to deliver concise, accurate findings.

Nuanced Reasoning: Thanks to its constitutional guardrails, Claude navigates complex ethical, technical, or creative prompts with greater care. It excels when you need step-by-step analysis or multiple viewpoints.

Scenario: You're evaluating two marketing strategies for a new product. Claude will weigh pros and cons, ask clarifying questions, and propose metrics to measure success rather than offering a one-line suggestion.

These strengths make Claude invaluable for deep-dive tasks that demand both breadth and depth.

CLAUDE VS. GPT: WHAT MAKES CLAUDE STAND OUT

At first glance, Claude and GPT may seem similar: both are advanced language models, both can write essays, code, or emails. Yet key differences emerge when you look closer:

1. **Focus on Alignment**
    - GPT models are highly creative and flexible

- Claude places stronger emphasis on safety and consistency

2. **Reliable Responses**
    - GPT may sometimes generate uncertain or incorrect information
    - Claude is more likely to acknowledge uncertainty and avoid speculation
3. **Structured Output**
    - Claude provides clearer and more structured responses
    - It maintains coherence even in longer explanations
4. **Reduced Hallucinations**
    - Claude generally produces fewer fabricated or misleading answers
    - It often encourages verification when needed

Key Insight: Claude is particularly valuable when **accuracy, clarity, and responsibility** are critical.

BEST USE CASES: ANALYSIS, SUMMARIZATION, DOCUMENT WORK, CODING

Claude is highly effective across several real-world applications:

1. **Analysis:** Evaluate business strategies, analyze reports and datasets, provide structured insights.
2. **Summarization:** Convert long documents into concise summaries, Extract key points from research papers and Generate meeting summaries.
3. **Document Work:** Review contracts and policies, Identify missing or unclear information and Draft professional reports.
4. **Coding:** Generate clean and structured code, Debug errors and Explain programming concepts.

These use cases highlight Claude's ability to handle complex, context-heavy tasks efficiently.

HANDS-ON: CRAFTING YOUR FIRST CLAUDE CONVERSATION

Ready to experience Claude firsthand? Follow these steps:

1. **Define Your Goal**
   - **Be specific:** "I need a 200-word summary of this 5-page PDF report on renewable energy policies."
2. **Prepare Your Prompt**

   "Claude, I'll paste a PDF summary below. Please extract the three main policy recommendations, provide one key statistic for each, and format your output as a numbered list."

3. **Provide Context**

   Include relevant text, data, or instructions.

4. **Ask Follow-Up Questions**

   Refine the output by asking: "Can you expand this section?", "Make the tone more formal."

5. **Iterate and Refine**

   Adjust your prompt until you get the desired result.

Key Tip: Clear instructions lead to better results.

CONCLUSION

Claude represents a new generation of AI systems one that combines advanced capabilities with a strong commitment to safety, honesty, and usefulness.

In this chapter, you learned:

- The vision behind Anthropic
- Claude's core principles
- Its unique strengths in reasoning and context understanding
- Key differences compared to other AI systems
- Practical ways to use Claude in real-world tasks

AI is not just about intelligence; it is about trust.

Claude demonstrates that AI can be both powerful and responsible.

As you continue your journey, you now have another valuable tool in your AI toolkit one that can help you think more clearly, work more efficiently, and make better decisions.

Start your first interaction with Claude and experience how a thoughtful AI assistant can transform the way you learn and work.

CHAPTER 7

GEMINI- GOOGLE'S MULTIMODAL POWERHOUSE

INTRODUCTION

Imagine managing multiple tasks at once responding to emails, analyzing spreadsheets, preparing presentations, and organizing ideas from handwritten notes. Now imagine having an intelligent assistant that can handle all of this seamlessly.

This is the promise of **Gemini,** Google's advanced AI system designed to transform how we interact with technology.

Unlike traditional AI tools that focus mainly on text, Gemini is built to understand and work with multiple types of information, including text, images, audio, and video. This makes it a powerful and flexible tool for both beginners and professionals.

In this chapter, you will learn:

- How Google's AI evolved from Bard to Gemini
- What multimodal AI means and why it is important
- The different versions of Gemini and their use cases
- How Gemini integrates with everyday tools
- Practical ways to use Gemini in real-world scenarios

By the end of this chapter, you will understand how Gemini can enhance your productivity, creativity, and decision-making.

GOOGLE'S AI JOURNEY: FROM BARD TO GEMINI

In 2021, Google introduced Bard: a text-based chatbot built on LaMDA's language prowess. While Bard demonstrated strong language capabilities, it had limitations in handling other types of data. To overcome these limitations, Google combined the expertise of its AI research teams, including Google DeepMind, to develop a more advanced system and the result was Gemini. Gemini works across multiple formats (text, images, audio, and video).

This evolution represents a shift from a single-purpose AI to a more comprehensive and intelligent system.

WHAT MULTIMODAL MEANS AND WHY IT MATTERS

The term *multimodal* simply means the ability to process and understand different types of input in a single system.

With Gemini, you can:

- Upload an image and ask questions about it
- Provide audio and request summaries
- Combine text and visuals for deeper insights

Examples:

- **Text + Image:** Convert handwritten notes into structured content
- **Audio + Text:** Transcribe and summarize a lecture
- **Video + Text:** Analyze a demonstration and extract key steps

Why It Is Important:

Multimodal AI reduces the need to switch between different tools. It allows you to interact with AI more naturally and efficiently. For beginners, this makes AI easier to use. For professionals, it significantly improves productivity and workflow efficiency.

GEMINI ULTRA, PRO, AND FLASH — WHICH VERSION FOR WHAT?

Gemini is available in different versions; each designed for specific use cases.

Gemini Ultra

- Highest capability and advanced reasoning
- Ideal for research, strategy, and complex problem-solving
- Best when accuracy and depth are critical

Gemini Pro

- Balanced performance and speed
- Suitable for everyday tasks such as writing, analysis, and communication
- Cost-effective for regular use

Gemini Flash

- Fast and efficient responses
- Ideal for quick questions and real-time interactions
- Useful for students and casual users

How to Choose:

- Use Ultra for deep analysis and complex tasks
- Use Pro for daily productivity

- Use Flash for quick and simple queries

DEEP INTEGRATION WITH GOOGLE WORKSPACE

Gemini isn't a standalone app; it's woven into the fabric of Google Workspace:

- **Gmail:** Draft and refine emails in moments. Upload a screenshot of technical notes, and Gemini crafts a clear summary for stakeholders.
- **Docs:** Expand ideas into full documents, generate summaries and explanations, add context to images and watch your document come alive.
- **Sheets:** Analyze data, generate charts and insights, Identify trends and patterns
- **Slides:** Upload a concept sketch and have Gemini generate polished slides, complete with speaker notes.
- **Meet:** Record your meeting, transcribe your meeting, extract action items, and send a follow-up summary automatically.

This seamless integration means AI assistance is just a click away, reducing friction and preserving your creative flow.

BEST USE CASES: RESEARCH, DATA, PRODUCTIVITY, SEARCH

1. **Research:** Summarize documents and reports, Compare different ideas or studies, Extract key insights
2. **Data Analysis:** Identify patterns in spreadsheets, explain data trends, Convert data into meaningful insights
3. **Productivity:** Automate repetitive tasks, organize schedules and tasks, Generate to-do lists
4. **Search:** Perform visual searches using images, ask contextual follow-up questions, Retrieve more accurate and relevant results

HANDS-ON: USING GEMINI IN YOUR DAILY WORKFLOW

Ready to make Gemini part of your routine? Follow these steps:

1. Enable Gemini in your Google account settings under "Labs."
2. Select your preferred version (Flash, Pro, or Ultra) based on your need.
3. **Craft clear prompts:**
    - **Begin with context:** "Here's a customer email screenshot..."

- **Specify the desired output:** "Please draft a response addressing concerns…"

4. **Use Multiple Inputs:** Upload images, text, or audio to get better results.
5. **Refine the output:** Ask follow-up questions such as:
   - "Can you simplify the language for a general audience?", "Make this simpler", "Add more details"
6. **Integrate into Apps:** Use Gemini within Gmail, Docs, Sheets, or Slides.

Treat Gemini as a collaborative partner. Provide clear instructions and refine your requests for better outcomes.

CONCLUSION

Gemini represents a giant leap in AI evolution—one that bridges text, visuals, and audio into a single, cohesive experience. Whether you're a total beginner exploring AI's potential or a seasoned professional seeking efficiency gain, Gemini empowers you to work smarter, think deeper, and create more dynamically than ever before. Embrace this multimodal powerhouse today: experiment boldly, integrate it into your daily tasks, and let Gemini propel you toward the next frontier of productivity and innovation.

The most important takeaway is this: **AI is becoming more natural, more intuitive, and more integrated into daily life.**

Gemini is not just a tool it is a powerful assistant that helps you think, create, and work more effectively.

As you continue your AI journey, explore Gemini hands-on. Experiment with different use cases, combine multiple inputs, and discover how it can enhance your productivity.

The future of AI is not limited to text it is multimodal, interactive, and deeply integrated into how we live and work.

And with tools like Gemini, that future is already here.

CHAPTER 8

GPT VS. CLAUDE VS. GEMINI-THE ULTIMATE COMPARISON

INTRODUCTION

Imagine you're about to hire an AI assistant, one that brainstorms blog posts, writes clean code, analyzes complex data, and keeps your sensitive information safe. With so many options, how do you pick the right one? In this chapter, we'll compare three of today's leading models OpenAI's GPT, Anthropic's Claude, and Google's Gemini against each other. You'll get a clear side-by-side comparison, learn which AI shines in writing, coding, reasoning, and safety, and discover a smart strategy for combining their strengths. By the end, you'll have the confidence to choose and even orchestrate all three like a pro.

SIDE-BY-SIDE CAPABILITY COMPARISON TABLE

Parameter	ChatGPT	Claude	Gemini
Creativity and Writing	Highly creative, excellent for storytelling and content creation	Structured and thoughtful writing	More factual and informative, less expressive
Accuracy and Reliability	Strong overall accuracy	More cautious and transparent	Highly reliable, especially with real-time data integration
Coding	Strong coding support and debugging	Excellent structured and well-documented code	Good, but slightly less consistent
Reasoning and Analysis	Strong general reasoning	Best for deep, multi-step reasoning	Excellent logical and structured responses
Context Handling	Large context support	Very high context understanding	Extremely large context (best for long documents)
Safety	Balanced safety and usability	Strongest safety and alignment	Strong moderation with flexibility
Integrations	Rich ecosystem with tools and plugins	Limited integrations	Deep integration with Google Workspace

WHICH AI IS BEST AT WRITING?

GPT is highly effective for storytelling, blog posts, creative writing or marketing content. Its knack for playful analogies, engaging hooks, and varied tone options makes it a favorite for content creators. Imagine you need a 1,500-word travel guide: GPT can adopt a friendly, conversational voice, sprinkle in vivid descriptions, and even suggest catchy titles and meta descriptions. Its huge user base means a wealth of community-created prompts and recipes to refine your output.

Claude is also strong, especially used for writing Professional documents, reports. It is used for more structured writing.

Gemini, benefiting from Google's vast language data. It performs well for Fact-based writing, Informational content and Multilingual tasks.

WHICH AI IS BEST FOR CODING?

For developers, GPT's specialized "code" models and Copilot integrations have made it a go-to. GPT can auto-complete functions, suggest unit tests, debug errors, and explain complex algorithms in plain English. Imagine you're stuck on a tricky recursion bug; GPT can offer a step-by-step explanation and alternative approaches.

Gemini also offers strong code assistance, with seamless ties to Google Cloud and Stack Overflow data. It's lightning-fast at retrieving code snippets and integrating with VS Code. Claude handles coding tasks solidly especially when you need safe, well-commented code with clear explanations. Overall, if you want the broadest plugin support and community resources, GPT tops the list, with Gemini close behind for Google ecosystem users.

WHICH AI IS BEST AT REASONING AND ANALYSIS?

When deep logical reasoning or data analysis is your goal, Claude often takes the crown. Trained with an emphasis on alignment and structured thinking, it excels at multi-step problem solving, brainstorming frameworks, and creating decision matrices. Picture a business analyst asking for a SWOT analysis of a new product: Claude can deliver a balanced, well-organized report with clear headings and bullet points.

GPT is strong too, especially its latest versions, which handle puzzles, legal reasoning prompts, and even mock interviews with flair.

Gemini, backed by Google's research, shows impressive performance on advanced reasoning benchmarks and statistical analysis. If you need the highest reliability in step-by-step logic, Claude leads;

for general smart responses, all three are competitive. For deep reasoning and structured thinking, Claude is often the top choice.

WHICH AI WINS AT SAFETY AND RELIABILITY?

Safety matters most when dealing with sensitive topics, regulated industries, or public-facing applications. Claude was built with safety as a core design principle, featuring guardrails that reduce harmful or biased outputs. It often asks clarifying questions if a prompt seems risky, making it ideal for healthcare summaries or HR policy drafts.

GPT has robust safety measures too, including content filters and red-team testing but sometimes needs carefully engineered prompts to avoid hallucinations.

Gemini benefits from Google's extensive content moderation infrastructure, delivering strong reliability in adhering to policies. For the highest built-in safety and alignment.

For sensitive or high-risk applications, Claude is the safest option, for balanced performance with configurable controls, GPT and Gemini are solid choices.

HOW TO CHOOSE THE RIGHT AI FOR YOUR SPECIFIC NEEDS

1. **Identify your priority:** creativity, code quality, reasoning depth, or safety.
2. **Match capabilities:**
   - Creative writing or marketing copy → GPT
   - Deep analysis or structured thinking → Claude
   - Real time data and Google integrations → Gemini
3. **Consider context length:** large reports or long chat histories may favor GPT-4 Turbo or Gemini.
4. **Weigh budget and access:** GPT has tiered pricing, Claude offers competitive rates, and Gemini is often bundled in Google Cloud plans.
5. **Test with pilot prompts:** run the same task across models to compare tone, accuracy, and speed before committing.

THE SMART APPROACH: USING ALL THREE STRATEGICALLY

Instead of choosing just one AI, you can combine their strengths.

Example Workflow:

- Use GPT for brainstorming ideas and writing drafts
- Use Gemini to validate facts and gather updated information
- Use Claude to structure the content and refine accuracy

Real-World Scenario:

For a market research report:

- GPT creates an engaging introduction
- Gemini provides the latest statistics
- Claude organizes the report and ensures clarity

CONCLUSION

Choosing between GPT, Claude, and Gemini does not have to be complicated.

Each system has its strengths:

- GPT excels in creativity and versatility
- Claude leads in reasoning, safety, and structured thinking
- Gemini stands out in integration and multimodal capabilities

The most important takeaway is this: **There is no single "best" AI, only the best AI for your specific needs.**

By understanding their differences and using them strategically, you can:

- Improve productivity
- Enhance creativity
- Make better decisions
- Stay ahead in the AI-driven world

As you continue your journey, experiment with these tools, combine their strengths, and discover what works best for you.

The future of AI is not about choosing one tool, it is about learning how to use them together effectively.

PART 3

PROMPTING MASTERY-TALK TO AI LIKE A PRO

"The quality of your output depends entirely on the quality of your input"

CHAPTER 9

THE ART AND SCIENCE OF PROMPTING

INTRODUCTION

In human conversations, the way we ask questions shapes the answers we receive. The same principle applies to Artificial Intelligence. A vague request leads to a vague response. A clear and thoughtful request leads to a precise and meaningful result. This happens more often than you might think, not because the AI lacks capability, but because the input it receives is unclear.

This is where **prompt engineering** comes in.

Prompting is more than just typing a question it is the skill of communicating effectively with AI. It is the bridge between your intention and the AI's output.

When done well, prompting transforms AI from a simple tool into a powerful assistant, creative partner, and problem-solving companion.

In this chapter, you will learn how to:

- Craft clear, structured, and effective prompts
- Understand how AI interprets your instructions
- Apply different prompting techniques for better results
- Avoid common mistakes that limit output quality
- Develop a practical approach to working with AI

By the end of this chapter, you will have the confidence to interact with AI systems more effectively and consistently achieve better outcomes.

WHAT IS PROMPT ENGINEERING AND WHY IT MATTERS

Prompt engineering is the process of designing inputs that guide AI systems to produce useful and accurate outputs. In simple terms, it is the ability to ask better questions.

As AI becomes part of everyday workflows like writing emails, generating ideas, analyzing data, and solving problems this skill becomes increasingly important.

Why Prompting Matters

- It improves the quality and relevance of responses
- It reduces time spent correcting or redoing outputs
- It helps you achieve your desired results more efficiently
- It allows you to fully leverage the capabilities of AI

A well-crafted prompt can turn a generic response into a highly tailored solution.

THE ANATOMY OF A PERFECT PROMPT

An effective prompt is not random; it follows a clear and structured approach. The best prompts typically include three key components:

CONTEXT: SETTING THE STAGE

Context provides background information so the AI understands the situation.

Example:

Instead of writing: "Write an email,"

You can write "You are a customer success manager at a SaaS company."

This immediately gives direction and clarity.

Task: Defining the Objective

Clearly state what you want the AI to do.

Example:

"Draft an email to a client who experienced a billing error and is frustrated. Apologize, explain the solution, and offer a small discount."

You've defined who, what, and why all vital for focused output.

Constraints: Setting the Rules

Add any constraints on tone, length, or format. Constraints define how the output should look.

Examples:

- "Use a friendly, empathetic tone."
- "Keep it under 150 words."
- "List action steps in bullet points."

Putting it all together, your prompt might look like this: "You are a customer success manager at a SaaS company. Draft an email to a client who experienced a billing error and is frustrated. Apologize sincerely, explain the corrective action, and offer a 10% discount. Use a friendly, empathetic tone and keep it under 150 words with bullet points for next steps."

ZERO-SHOT, ONE-SHOT, AND FEW-SHOT PROMPTING EXPLAINED

Different situations require different prompting strategies. Understanding these techniques will help you improve consistency and accuracy.

Zero-Shot Prompting

You provide instructions without examples.

- **Example:** "Translate the following sentence into French: 'The weather is lovely today.'"
- **Pros:** Quick and simple.
- **Cons:** May yield less consistent results on complex tasks.

One-Shot Prompting

You include a single example to demonstrate desired output.

- **Prompt:** "Example – English: 'I love cooking.' French: 'J'adore cuisiner.'
- **Now translate:** 'The cat is sleeping on the sofa.'"
- **Pros:** Shows AI exactly what format and style you expect.
- **Cons:** Limited scope; might not cover edge cases.

Few-Shot Prompting

You provide multiple examples before asking the model to perform the task.

Prompt:

- **Example 1 – English:** 'The sky is blue.' French: 'Le ciel est bleu.'
- **Example 2 – English:** 'She reads every night.' French: 'Elle lit chaque soir.'
- **Now translate:** 'He travels to Japan every year.'"
- **Pros:** Higher accuracy and consistency.
- **Cons:** Uses more tokens, can be slower or costlier on paid APIs.

Choose the approach that balances precision against simplicity and cost. For quick tasks, zero-shot often suffices. For critical or complex outputs, few-shot shines.

COMMON PROMPTING MISTAKES BEGINNERS MAKE

Even small mistakes in prompting can reduce the quality of results. Being aware of these will help you improve quickly.

1. **Being Too Vague:** Vague prompts lead to unclear responses.

Instead of: "Write a summary"

Use: "Write a 100-word summary for business executives focusing on key insights."

2. **Overloading the Prompt:** Trying to include too many instructions at once can confuse the AI.

   Solution: Break tasks into smaller steps.

3. **Assuming AI Understands Your Intent:** AI does not automatically know your expectations. Always specify: Tone, Format and Purpose

4. **Not Iterating:** The first response is rarely perfect. Refine your prompt and improve the output step by step.

5. **Ignoring Limitations:** AI systems have limits in handling very large inputs.

   Solution: Break long content into smaller sections and focus on key parts.

By recognizing these mistakes and applying the fixes, you'll accelerate your learning curve and get more reliable results from every interaction.

Practical Strategies for Better Prompting

To consistently get high-quality results, follow these best practices:

- Be clear, specific, and intentional
- Use structured prompts (context + task + constraints)

- Provide examples when needed
- Break complex tasks into smaller steps
- Treat prompting as an interactive process

CONCLUSION: TURNING SCIENCE INTO ART

Prompt engineering is both a science and an art.

It requires:

- Clear thinking
- Structured communication
- Creative problem-solving

In this chapter, you have learned how to:

- Build effective prompts
- Apply different prompting techniques
- Avoid common mistakes
- Improve your interaction with AI

The most important takeaway is this: **The quality of your output depends on the quality of your input.**

By mastering prompting, you move from simply using AI to collaborating with it effectively.

As you continue your journey, experiment with different prompt styles, refine your approach, and observe how small changes can lead to significantly better results.

With practice, prompting becomes second nature and AI becomes a powerful partner in learning, working, and creating.

In the next chapter, you will explore advanced prompting techniques that will further enhance your ability to work with AI systems and unlock their full potential.

CHAPTER 10

ADVANCED PROMPTING TECHNIQUES

INTRODUCTION: LEVELING UP YOUR AI CONVERSATIONS

By now, you understand how to communicate with AI using clear and structured prompts. But what if you could take your results to the next level making them more precise, more insightful, and more aligned with your goals?

This is where **advanced prompting techniques** come into play.

Think of basic prompting as asking questions. Advanced prompting, on the other hand, is about **guiding the conversation strategically.**

Instead of hoping for the right answer, you begin to:

- Shape how the AI thinks
- Control how it responds
- Refine outputs step by step

Whether you are a student, professional, or curious learner, these techniques will help you unlock the full potential of AI.

In this chapter, you will explore:

- Chain-of-thought prompting
- Role-based prompting
- Iterative prompting
- Prompt templates for real-world tasks
- Building your own prompt library

By the end of this chapter, you will move from being a user of AI to becoming a **skilled AI collaborator.**

CHAIN-OF-THOUGHT PROMPTING

What Is Chain-of-Thought Prompting?

Chain-of-thought prompting guides the AI to break down its reasoning step by step, just as you would explain your thought process to someone else. This technique encourages transparency, reduces errors, and produces more logical, comprehensive answers.

Why It Matters

- Improves logical accuracy
- Reduces incorrect or misleading responses
- Makes reasoning transparent and easier to verify
- Ideal for complex tasks such as analysis, planning, and problem-solving

How to Use It

- **Frame the Task:** "Let's solve this step by step."
- **Prompt for Reasoning:** "List each consideration you'd make."
- **Request a Conclusion:** "After those steps, what's the final answer?"

Example

Prompt: We need to budget $10,000 across marketing, development, and operations. Explain your reasoning step by step, then give me the recommended budget allocation.

AI Response (chain-of-thought):

- Identify core goals…
- Estimate costs…
- Allocate funds…

Final allocation: Marketing $4,000; Development $3,500; Operations $2,500.

ROLE-BASED PROMPTING: GIVING AI A PERSONA

What Is Role-Based Prompting?

You instruct the AI to adopt a specific role like an expert chef, a financial advisor, or a marketing manager so it responds with the tone, knowledge level, and style of that role.

Benefits

- Leverages contextual expertise and jargon.
- Creates consistency in style and format.
- Makes the conversation feel more natural and targeted.

How to Use It

- **Define the Role:** "You are a senior UX designer."
- **Specify the Task:** "Explain best practices for mobile onboarding."
- **Add Constraints:** "Keep it under 300 words and use layman's terms."

Example

Prompt: You are a career coach with 10 years of experience. Advise a recent graduate on how to network effectively on LinkedIn.

AI Response:

- Craft a professional headline.
- Personalize connection requests…
- Engage with relevant posts…

ITERATIVE PROMPTING: REFINING OUTPUTS STEP BY STEP

What Is Iterative Prompting?

Iterative prompting is the process of improving results through multiple rounds of interaction. Instead of expecting a perfect answer in one attempt, you refine the output gradually. You guide the AI through multiple refinements: initial draft, feedback, tweaks, and final polish.

Why It's Powerful

- Mimics a collaborative editing process.
- Each iteration hones clarity, tone, and accuracy.
- Prevents overwhelming the AI with too many instructions at once.

How to Use It

- **Start with a basic request:** "Write a quick overview."
- **Review the output:** "Make it more conversational."
- **Provide feedback:** "Add a real-world example."
- **Refine and improve:** "Shorten to 150 words."

Example Workflow

- **Prompt:** "Draft a cold-email script for outreach to marketing directors."
- **AI Draft:** Basic email.
- **You:** "Add a subject line and make it friendlier."
- **AI Revision:** Subject line + warmer tone.
- **You:** "Include a call-to-action and reduce word count."
- **Final Email:** Crisp, action-oriented, under 120 words.

PROMPT TEMPLATES FOR COMMON PROFESSIONAL TASKS

Why Templates Matter

Having ready-made prompts saves time and ensures consistency. Instead of reinventing the wheel, you adapt proven templates to each situation.

Sample Templates

1. **Meeting Agenda Builder**
    - **Prompt:** "Create a 30-minute meeting agenda for a product launch review, including objectives, talking points, and time allocations."
2. **Market Research Summary**
    - **Prompt:** "Summarize the latest trends in remote work tools, highlighting three key findings and their implications for small businesses."
3. **Social Media Calendar**
    - **Prompt:** "Generate a two-week Instagram content calendar for a health-food brand, including captions and hashtag suggestions."
4. **Project Risk Assessment**
    - **Prompt:** "List five potential risks for a website redesign project and propose mitigation strategies for each."
5. **Press Release Draft**
    - **Prompt:** "Write a 200-word press release announcing our new AI feature, focusing on benefits for end users and a quote from the CEO."

How to Customize Templates

- Swap industry details ("health-food" to "edtech").
- Adjust word counts or formats (bullet list vs. paragraph).
- Add or remove sections (e.g., "Include budget estimates").

BUILDING YOUR PERSONAL PROMPT LIBRARY

Why a Prompt Library?

As you continue using AI, you will discover prompts, templates, and role definitions that work exceptionally well and streamline your workflow. A prompt library helps you store, organize, and reuse these prompts. It saves time, improve consistency, build a personal workflow system, help to track what work best.

Steps to Create and Maintain Your Library

- **Organize prompt by Category:** Separate marketing, HR, coding, research, etc.
- **Name Your Prompts Clearly:** "Email Outreach Friendly Tone."
- **Track Improvement and Version Control:** Note dates and tweaks made in each iteration.

- **Note Effectiveness and Result:** Record success metrics, time saved, user feedback, quality of output.
- **Share and Collaborate with your team:** If you work in a team, use a shared doc or wiki so everyone benefits.

Example Entry

- **Title:** "Annual Report Summary"
- **Category:** Corporate Communications
- **Prompt:** "You are a financial analyst. Summarize our Q4 earnings report in 250 words, emphasizing growth drivers and challenges."
- **Version:** v2.1 (Updated tone to be more optimistic)

Notes: "Worked best when followed by a chain-of-thought prompt for verifying figures."

CONCLUSION

Advanced prompting techniques take your AI skills from basic usage to strategic mastery.

In this chapter, you learned how to:

- Guide AI reasoning with chain-of-thought prompting

- Use role-based prompts for more relevant responses
- Refine outputs through iterative prompting
- Save time using prompt templates
- Build a personal prompt library for long-term efficiency

The key takeaway is this: **The more thoughtfully you guide AI, the more powerful it becomes.**

As you continue practicing these techniques, you will notice a significant improvement in the quality, clarity, and usefulness of your results.

Start small. Experiment with one technique at a time. Observe the differences. Refine your approach.

Over time, you will develop your own prompting style and that is where true mastery begins.

In the next chapter, we will explore how to measure, evaluate, and optimize AI-driven workflows to ensure consistent and high-quality results.

CHAPTER 11

PROMPTING GPT, CLAUDE & GEMINI DIFFERENTLY

INTRODUCTION

Every time you ask GPT, Claude or Gemini the same question, you might be surprised by how different their answers can be. It's like ordering the same dish at three different restaurants. Each chef uses different ingredients, techniques, and styles so even though the request is the same, the result feels unique. The same applies to AI systems like ChatGPT, Claude, and Gemini. Each model has been designed differently. They are trained on different data, guided by different principles, and optimized for different strengths.

In this chapter, we'll explore why identical prompts yield different outputs, and how you can fine-tune your requests to get the best from each model. Whether you're a complete beginner, a curious learner or a working professional, you'll learn simple adjustments you can make right now to transform vague requests into powerful, precise prompts.

WHY THE SAME PROMPT GIVES DIFFERENT RESULTS ACROSS MODELS

At first glance, all large language models seem similar: they process text and generate humanlike responses. Under the hood, however, each model has been trained on different data, tuned with different objectives, and optimized for different strengths.

1. **Training Data and Objectives**

    - GPT (from OpenAI) is designed for creativity, flexibility, and conversational fluency.
    - Claude (from Anthropic) focuses on safety, clarity, and structured responses.
    - Gemini (from Google) emphasizes reasoning, factual accuracy, and real-world data.

    Because of these differences, the same prompt can lead to very different styles of answers.

2. **Built-in Rules and Safety Systems**

    Each AI model follows its own internal guidelines (often called system rules or guardrails).

    - Claude tends to be more cautious and explanatory

- GPT balances creativity with usability
- Gemini often prioritizes factual and structured responses

These built-in behaviors influence tone, depth, and format.

3. **Response Style and Output Behavior**

   Even when answering the same question:

   - GPT may provide a creative and engaging explanation
   - Claude may deliver a structured and careful response
   - Gemini may offer a more analytical and data-driven answer

Understanding these differences helps you guide each model more effectively.

TAILORING PROMPTS FOR GPT'S STRENGTHS

GPT shines when you give it clear, structured requests and the flexibility to explore creatively. Here's how to leverage its advantages:

1. **Use a Clear Persona or Role**

   Example: "You are a friendly marketing guru with expertise in wellness products. Draft a 150-

word social media caption about the benefits of meditation for beginners."

By specifying role, style and length, GPT will adopt that voice.

2. **Break Tasks into Steps**

   Example:

   Step 1: List five benefits of meditation.

   Step 2: For each benefit, provide a one-sentence example scenario.

   Step 3: Write a short conclusion inviting readers to try a simple meditation."

   GPT loves multi-part instructions and will follow them sequentially.

3. **Specify Formatting and Tone**

   Example: "Use a friendly and conversational tone"

   GPT will pay attention to these details to match your desired style.

4. **Adjust Temperature for Creativity**

   If you need brainstorming or creative slogans, set temperature to 0.7–1.0.

For factual summaries or code, drop it to 0.2–0.5.

TAILORING PROMPTS FOR CLAUDE'S STRENGTHS

Claude is designed for safe, thoughtful outputs and excels at summarization and structured responses:

1. **Leverage the "Assistant Style" Parameter**

   Example: "CLAUDE: respond as a concise, friendly coach. Provide bullet points only."

   Claude will adopt the specified style and stick to bullets if asked.

2. **Ask for Ethical or Safety Considerations**

   Example: "Summarize the health benefits of meditation, and note any common misconceptions or precautions."

   Claude's guardrails ensure it highlights potential risks or caveats you might overlook.

3. **Use Context Windows Smartly**

   Claude often allows long context windows.

   Example: "Here's my chapter draft (2,000 words). Provide a 200-word executive summary."

4. **Request Structured Outputs**

   Example: "Create a table with three columns: Benefit, Description, Example. Populate with five benefits of meditation."

   Claude will reliably produce neat tables.

Example Prompt for Claude: "List five benefits of meditation in bullet points. Include one caution. Keep each point under 15 words."

TAILORING PROMPTS FOR GEMINI'S STRENGTHS

Gemini integrates Google's retrieval, logic and multimodal prowess. Use these tips to maximize its unique capabilities:

1. **Invoke Real-Time or Factual Retrieval**

   Example: "Using the latest research, summarize three recent studies (2023–2024) on meditation's impact on stress."

   If retrieval is enabled, Gemini will cite sources and up-to-date findings.

2. **Incorporate Multimodal Inputs (where supported)**

   Example: "Here's a chart showing weekly meditation minutes. Analyze trends and recommend improvements."

   Gemini can parse that chart image and comment intelligently.

3. **Ask for Detailed Reasoning**

   Example: "Explain step-by-step why meditation can reduce cortisol levels, including biochemical mechanisms."

Gemini's strength in logic and reasoning shines through deeper, more technical explanations.

4. **Use Google-Style Prompts**

   Example: "Define: meditation benefits site:.edu OR site:.gov."

   Mimicking search operators can help Gemini fetch or simulate source-backed content.

REAL-WORLD PROMPT EXAMPLES WITH ACTUAL OUTPUTS COMPARED

Below is a simple prompt we'll feed to all three models, followed by tailored versions and sample outputs. Notice the differences and the impact of our tweaks.

Prompt A (Generic):

"Write a summary of the benefits of meditation."

GPT Output A (approximate):

"Meditation offers numerous benefits. It reduces stress by calming the mind, improves concentration by training focus, enhances emotional well-being by promoting self-awareness, and can lower blood pressure through relaxation. Regular practice may also support better sleep, increase empathy, and foster resilience to life's challenges."

Claude Output A (approximate):

Meditation Benefits Summary:

- **Stress Reduction:** Short-term calming effect and long-term emotional resilience.
- **Enhanced Focus:** Improves attention span and task performance.
- **Emotional Balance:** Encourages self-reflection and reduces anxiety.
- **Physical Health:** Lowers blood pressure and supports cardiovascular health.
- **Improved Sleep:** Promotes relaxation before bedtime."

Gemini Output A (approximate):

"Meditation positively impacts mental and physical health. According to a 2023 meta-analysis, regular practice reduces cortisol levels by up to 20%, improves attention by 15%, and decreases risk of hypertension. It fosters neural plasticity in the prefrontal cortex, leading to better decision-making and emotional regulation."

Prompt B (Tailored for GPT):

"You are a wellness blogger. Write a 100-word, conversational summary of meditation benefits, using a personal anecdote and ending with a question to engage readers."

GPT Output B (approximate):

"As someone who struggled with constant stress, I discovered that just ten minutes of daily meditation felt like hitting the reset button for my mind. Meditation helped me notice the rise and fall of my thoughts, leading to clearer focus, lower anxiety and more restful sleep. It's like giving your brain a mini-vacation every day. How might you feel after trying this yourself?"

Prompt C (Tailored for Claude):

"CLAUDE: In bullet points, list five benefits of meditation, include one caution, and keep each point under 15 words."

Claude Output C (approximate):

- Reduces stress levels.
- Improves attention span.
- Balances emotions.
- Lowers blood pressure.
- Enhances sleep quality.

Caution: Start slowly to avoid frustration."

Prompt D (Tailored for Gemini):

"Using recent studies, list three scientifically validated benefits of meditation, cite the study year and source."

Gemini Output D (approximate):

- **Stress Reduction:** 2023 Journal of Clinical Psychology -20% cortisol decrease.
- **Attention Improvement:** 2024 Cognitive Science Review –15% boost in sustained focus.
- **Sleep Quality:** 2023 Sleep Medicine Journal – 30% fewer nighttime awakenings."

By adjusting our prompts, we guide each model toward its strengths whether it's GPT's creativity, Claude's safety and structure, or Gemini's factual retrieval and reasoning.

CONCLUSION

Learning to prompt GPT, Claude, and Gemini effectively is like learning to work with three different experts. Each has its own strengths. The key to success is not just choosing the right tool but knowing how to communicate with each one effectively.

The most important takeaway is this: **The same question can produce very different results depending on how and where you ask it.**

As you continue your journey try to experiment with different prompts, observe how each model responds and adapt your approach based on the task to get the best result.

With practice, you will develop the ability to get the best out of any AI system.

PART 4

AI IN ACTION-REAL WORLD APPLICATIONS

"AI is only as valuable as what you do with it"

CHAPTER 12
AI FOR PERSONAL PRODUCTIVITY

INTRODUCTION

In today's fast-paced world, it often feels like there is never enough time. Emails keep arriving. Meetings fill up the calendar. To-do lists keep growing. And despite our best efforts, staying organized and productive can feel overwhelming.

Now imagine having a smart assistant one that helps you manage tasks, organize your schedule, summarize information, and even support your learning.

This is where **Artificial Intelligence for personal productivity** comes in.

AI is no longer just for businesses or developers. It is now part of everyday life, helping individuals work smarter, save time, and focus on what truly matters.

In this chapter, you will discover how AI can:

- Simplify daily tasks
- Improve time management
- Enhance learning and knowledge retention
- Support your personal and professional growth

Whether you are a student, a professional, or someone looking to stay organized, AI can become your most valuable productivity partner.

MANAGING EMAILS, CALENDARS, AND TASKS WITH AI

Daily administrative work like emails, scheduling, and task tracking can consume a significant amount of time. AI tools can handle many of these repetitive tasks efficiently.

Smart Email Assistants

AI-powered email tools can help you write, reply, and manage messages faster.

Common features include:

- Auto-suggestions while typing
- One-click reply options
- Follow-up reminders
- Priority inbox sorting

Instead of spending time drafting routine responses, AI can suggest complete sentences or quick replies, allowing you to respond in seconds. Over time, these small-time savings add up significantly.

Calendar Optimization

Managing your schedule manually can be frustrating, especially when priorities change.

AI-powered calendar tools can:

- Automatically find the best meeting times
- Rearrange low-priority events
- Create focus blocks for deep work
- Avoid scheduling conflicts

For example, if your day is filled with meetings, AI can identify gaps and create uninterrupted time for important tasks. This helps you stay productive without constantly adjusting your calendar.

Automated Task Management

AI tools can also help you organize and prioritize your tasks.

Features include:

- Smart task suggestions
- Automatic deadlines and reminders
- Workflow automation

For example, when you add a task like "Prepare project report," AI can suggest:

- A priority level
- A due date
- Related subtasks

This reduces mental load and helps you stay focused on execution rather than planning.

AI-POWERED NOTE-TAKING AND SUMMARIZATION

Whether you're in a meeting, attending a lecture, or conducting research, capturing and understanding information is critical. AI note-taking tools can record, transcribe, and generate concise summaries, complete with action items and highlights.

Real-Time Transcription

AI tools can record and convert conversations into text instantly. This allows you to focus on the discussion instead of taking notes, review conversations later and search for key topics quickly. Imagine attending a meeting without worrying about missing important details AI captures everything for you.

Intelligent Summaries

AI can analyze large amounts of information and generate concise summaries.

For example:

- Convert long meeting notes into key takeaways
- Summarize articles or research papers
- Highlight important points

Instead of reading pages of content, you can quickly understand the most important insights.

Extracting Action Items

AI goes beyond summarization; it identifies tasks and responsibilities.

For example:

- "Follow up with client"
- "Prepare presentation slides"
- "Submit report by Friday"

These can be automatically converted into tasks, ensuring nothing is missed.

LEARNING FASTER WITH AI AS YOUR TUTOR

AI is transforming how we learn. Instead of relying only on traditional methods, you can now interact with AI as a personalized tutor. AI tutors adapt to your pace and style.

Conversational Q&A

AI tools can explain complex topics in simple terms, provide real-life examples and answer follow-up questions.

If you do not understand something, you can ask for a simpler explanation, a step-by-step breakdown and additional examples. This creates a highly personalized learning experience.

Adaptive Practice

AI-powered learning platforms adjust based on your performance. They can Identify weak areas, Provide targeted exercises and Reinforce learning through repetition. This makes learning more efficient and focused.

Personalized Learning Paths

AI platforms analyze your progress, identify gaps, and recommend the next modules or resources. Instead of following a fixed curriculum, you get a customized learning journey that adapts to your needs.

AI TOOLS FOR EVERYDAY LIFE

AI can boost productivity beyond work and study. Everyday tasks from meal planning to fitness tracking are prime candidates for intelligent assistance.

Virtual Assistants and Shortcuts

- Apple's Siri Shortcuts automate multi-step routines on your iPhone
- Google Assistant routines trigger actions like "Good morning" (lights on, news brief, calendar overview)

With a single voice command or tap, Siri can brew your preferred coffee via a smart maker, turn off your alarm, and read out today's top headlines. Google Assistant can dim lights, set the thermostat, get weather update and remind you of dinner reservations before you've even left the couch.

Meal Planning and Grocery Lists

- Paprika Recipe Manager suggests dinner ideas based on ingredients you have
- AnyList's AI categorizes grocery items and auto-sorts them by aisle

Tell Paprika you have chicken breasts, spinach, and rice. It crafts recipe suggestions, updates your meal plan, and builds a shopping list of missing ingredients. AnyList then groups items by store layout, so your weekly grocery run becomes a breeze.

Health, Fitness, and Budgeting

- MyFitnessPal's AI predicts calorie needs and suggests meals

- Fitbod's AI tailors' gym routines to your progress and equipment availability
- Cleo and Trim's AI bots analyze spending habits and propose savings goals

Whether you're tracking macros, lifting weights, or managing finances, AI tools spot patterns you might miss. They celebrate your milestones, remind you of looming deadlines (for bills or workouts), and adapt recommendations as your habits evolve.

CONCLUSION

Artificial Intelligence is transforming personal productivity in ways that were once unimaginable. It is not about replacing human effort it is about enhancing it.

In this chapter, you learned how AI can:

- Manage emails, calendars, and tasks
- Capture and summarize information
- Support faster and smarter learning
- Improve everyday life activities

The most important takeaway is this: **AI gives you back your most valuable resource and time.**

Start small:

- Use AI to manage emails
- Try AI-powered note-taking

- Experiment with a virtual assistant

As you grow more comfortable, you can gradually integrate more tools into your daily routine.

Over time, AI becomes more than just a tool, it becomes a trusted partner in your personal and professional journey.

In the next chapter, we will explore on AI for Business and Professional.

CHAPTER 13

AI FOR BUSINESS AND PROFESSIONALS

INTRODUCTION

In today's competitive world, businesses are constantly searching for ways to work faster, smarter, and more efficiently. Artificial Intelligence (AI) is no longer a futuristic concept it is a practical tool that is already transforming how organizations operate across industries. From automating routine tasks to uncovering valuable insights hidden in data, AI is helping businesses make better decisions and achieve greater results.

Whether you are a beginner exploring AI for the first time or a professional looking to stay relevant or a business owner aiming to gain a competitive advantage understanding how AI applies to real-world business scenarios is essential.

In this chapter, you will learn how AI is transforming Marketing, Finance, Human Resources (HR), Customer Service and Specialized industries such as healthcare, legal, and education.

By the end of this chapter, you will have a clear understanding of how AI can drive productivity, innovation, and growth in professional environments.

AI IN MARKETING: CONTENT, SEO, AND SOCIAL MEDIA

Marketing is one of the areas where AI has had the most visible impact. AI-powered tools can help businesses create content, optimize search engine performance, and manage social media more effectively.

Content Creation

AI tools can generate Blog posts, email campaigns, social media captions, advertising copy and many more. Instead of starting from scratch, marketers can use AI to Generate ideas, create drafts and Refine messaging.

This significantly reduces the time required to produce high-quality content.

Search Engine Optimization (SEO)

AI helps improve website visibility by analyzing Keywords, Competitor content and Search trends. It can recommend Content structure, Relevant topics and Keyword placement. This allows businesses to create content that ranks higher on search engines.

Social Media Management

AI tools can Schedule posts at optimal times, suggest hashtags, analyze audience engagement and Identify trending topics. This helps businesses connect with their audience more effectively and increase engagement.

AI IN FINANCE: ANALYSIS, FORECASTING, AND REPORTING

Finance relies heavily on data, and AI excels at processing and analyzing large amounts of information. For data analysis AI can quickly identify Patterns, Anomalies and Trends. Imagine uploading last quarter's spreadsheets into a platform like Microsoft Power BI or Tableau augmented with AI. Within seconds, the system spots anomalies a sudden spike in expenses or an underperforming sales region and surfaces them in an interactive dashboard.

Forecasting gets a major upgrade with machine learning models. AI models can predict Future revenue, Cash flow and Market trends. Rather than rely on static growth rates, AI tools can ingest historical sales, seasonal trends, and even external indicators like commodity prices or social media buzz. QuickBooks' AI-driven forecasting, for example, predicts cash flow with alarming accuracy, helping small businesses plan for lean months or invest surplus funds wisely.

In case of **automated reporting**, AI can generate reports that include Visual dashboards, Written summaries and Insights and recommendations. Tools like IBM Watson Analytics or TIBCO Spotfire auto-generate narrative summaries. You receive a weekly PDF that not only charts revenue trends but explains them: "Revenue fell 8% in the Northeast region this month, likely due to supply chain delays impacting product B." This frees finance teams to focus on strategy instead of wrestling with spreadsheets.

AI IN HR: RECRUITMENT, ONBOARDING, AND TRAINING

AI is transforming how organizations hire, train, and manage employees.

Recruitment

AI tools can Screen resumes, Match candidates to job roles and Rank applicants based on suitability. AI-driven applicant tracking systems like LinkedIn

Recruiter and HireVue screen resumes for relevant skills, highlight promising candidates, and even schedule interviews automatically. Instead of sifting through hundreds of resumes, you review a shortlist of top matches ranked by predictive success scores. This speeds up the hiring process and improves decision-making.

Onboarding

AI chatbots can Guide new employees, answer common questions and assist with documentation, guide employees through paperwork, answer FAQs about company policies, and set up initial training schedules. A chatbot might remind John in marketing to complete his cybersecurity module, while also directing new hires to the employee portal for benefits enrollment. This creates a smoother onboarding experience.

Training and Development

AI platforms provide Personalized learning recommendations, Skill development paths and Performance insights. Employees can learn at their own pace, improving both productivity and job satisfaction. Training and professional development go personalized with platforms like Coursera for Business or Degreed, which use machine learning to recommend courses based on an employee's role, past performance, and career aspirations

AI IN CUSTOMER SERVICE: CHATBOTS AND AUTOMATION

Customer expectations have changed people now expect quick and accurate responses. AI helps businesses meet these expectations.

Chatbots

AI-powered chatbots can Answer common questions, handle routine requests and provide instant support. This reduces workload on human agents.

Intelligent Support Systems

AI can Analyze customer sentiment, Route queries to the right team and Suggest responses to agents. This improves efficiency and customer satisfaction.

Automation

AI automates repetitive tasks such as Ticket assignment, Follow-up reminders, Issue tracking, hospital appointment booking system, opening bank account, front desk executive, email automation and many more. This allows support teams to focus on complex problems.

Customers expect immediate, accurate support around the clock and AI chatbots deliver. Tools like Zendesk's Answer Bot or Intercom's Resolution Bot handle up to 50% of routine inquiries password resets, order status checks, and billing questions without human intervention. When conversations require empathy or complex troubleshooting, bots seamlessly hand off to live agents, complete with conversation history and suggested responses.

Sentiment analysis engines scan chats and social media mention in real time, alerting managers to unhappy customers before a small issue escalates into a public relations headache. If a customer tweets frustration about a delayed shipment, your AI dashboard flags the mention, prompts a proactive apology, and triggers a discounted shipping offer.

Beyond chat, AI automates ticket routing by skill set and workload. High-priority issues go to your most experienced reps, while simple queries go to newcomers for on-the-job training. This intelligent triage reduces response times, improves customer satisfaction, and lets your support team focus on solving problems rather than juggling assignments.

AI IN SPECIALIZED INDUSTRIES: HEALTHCARE, LEGAL, AND EDUCATION SECTORS

AI is also transforming industries beyond traditional business functions.

Healthcare

In health care AI can Assist in diagnosis, Analyze medical images and Support patient care. This improves accuracy and helps doctors make better decisions. Imagine virtual assistants triaging patients before they ever step into a clinic. Babylon Health and Ada Health use conversational AI to ask symptom-based questions, prioritize cases, and schedule telemedicine visits. Meanwhile, diagnostic support tools like Google DeepMind's AI for eye disease analyze retinal scans with accuracy rivaling specialists—catching issues earlier and saving lives.

Legal

In legal AI tools help with Contract analysis, Legal research and Document review. This reduces time spent on repetitive tasks. Contract review and legal research often involve sifting through thousands of pages. AI platforms like ROSS Intelligence and Legal Robot apply natural language processing to summarize contracts, highlight risky clauses, and even suggest alternative wording. Lawyers can now spend more time crafting strategy and less time on routine document analysis.

Education

In education AI supports Personalized learning, Adaptive assessments and Student performance tracking. This enhances both teaching and learning experiences. Personalized learning platforms such as Khan Academy's AI-powered tutor or Coursera's adaptive quizzes tailor lessons to each student's strengths and weaknesses. If a learner struggles with quadratic equations, the system provides extra practice problems and video tutorials on demand. Teachers gain actionable insights into class performance, enabling targeted interventions where they matter most.

Across these specialized fields, AI accelerates workflows, reduces errors, and elevates human expertise. By handling repetitive tasks and delivering data-driven insights, AI frees professionals to focus on strategic, creative, and empathetic work.

The Bigger Impact of AI in Business

Across all industries, AI delivers three key benefits:

1. **Efficiency:** Automates repetitive tasks and saves time

2. **Insight:** Analyzes data to provide actionable recommendations
3. **Innovation:** Enables new products, services, and business models

AI allows professionals to focus on higher-value work such as strategy, creativity, and decision-making.

CONCLUSION

Artificial Intelligence is transforming the way businesses and professionals operate. It is not just about automation it is about **enhancing human potential.**

In this chapter, you learned how AI is:

- Improving marketing strategies
- Enhancing financial decision-making
- Streamlining HR processes
- Transforming customer service
- Driving innovation across industries

The most important takeaway is this: **AI is not replacing professionals it is empowering them.**

To get started:

- Identify areas where AI can save time
- Experiment with simple tools
- Start with small projects

- Measure results and scale gradually

As you continue your journey, think of AI as a partner, one that helps you work smarter, make better decisions, and unlock new opportunities.

The future of work is not just human or AI, it is **human + AI working together.**

CHAPTER 14
AI FOR DEVELOPERS AND TECH PROFESSIONALS

INTRODUCTION

Imagine having a coding partner who never gets tired, helps you automate repetitive tasks instantly suggests solutions, and helps you debug problems in seconds. This is no longer imagination it is the reality of **Artificial Intelligence in software development.**

AI is transforming how developers write code, build applications, and manage systems. Tasks that once took hours such as debugging, documentation, and testing can now be completed in minutes with the help of AI tools.

Whether you are A beginner learning to code, A developer looking to improve productivity or a tech professional exploring the future of software engineering. AI offers powerful opportunities to work smarter and build faster.

In this chapter, you will learn:

- How AI assists in coding and development
- How to automate workflows using AI APIs
- How to build your first AI-powered application
- How to integrate AI into existing systems
- What the future of software development looks like

By the end of this chapter, you will have a clear understanding of how to use AI as a practical tool in your development workflow.

AI-ASSISTED CODING WITH GITHUB COPILOT, CLAUDE CODE, AND GPT

AI-assisted coding tools act like real-time collaborators, use machine learning to predict your next lines of code, debug errors, and generate documentation on the fly. They help you write, improve, and understand code more efficiently.

Let's look at three leading assistants:

1. **GitHub Copilot:** It Provides real-time code suggestions, completes functions and repetitive code and integrates with popular IDEs like VS

Code. Trained on billions of lines of public code .When you type, it predicts what you want to write next, saving time on boilerplate code.

2. **Claude Code:** Focuses on safe and structured code, Helps explain complex logic and Generates test cases and documentation. Built by Anthropic with guardrails to prevent insecure patterns. It is especially useful when you need clear explanations and reliable outputs.
3. **GPT (via OpenAI):** ChatGPT is flexible and prompt-driven, can generate, refactor, and debug code and supports multiple programming languages. You can ask it to Explain code, convert between languages and Suggest improvements

Best Practices for AI-Assisted Coding

- Provide clear comments and context
- Review AI-generated code carefully
- Test for edge cases and security issues
- Combine multiple tools for better results

AI is a powerful assistant but human oversight remains essential.

AUTOMATING WORKFLOWS WITH AI APIS

AI is not limited to writing code it can also automate development workflows.

Beyond autocompletion, AI APIs let you embed intelligence into your build, testing, and deployment pipelines. Consider these practical automations:

1. **Generating Release Notes:** AI can analyze commit history and create user-friendly summaries. This saves time and ensures consistent documentation.
2. **Code Documentation:** AI can automatically generate function descriptions, API documentation and README files. This keeps documentation updated without manual effort.
3. **Ticket Triage and Summaries:** AI can Summarize issues, assign priorities and categorize tasks. This improves team productivity and communication. Connect your issue tracker (Jira, GitHub Issues) to an AI endpoint.

Getting started with AI APIs:

1. Choose an AI platform (e.g., OpenAI or similar)
2. Identify a repetitive task in your workflow.
3. Write a small automation script or CI job that sends relevant data to the AI endpoint.

4. Test, refine prompts, and monitor usage to keep costs in check.

BUILDING YOUR FIRST AI-POWERED APPLICATION

Creating an AI-powered application is easier than ever. Let's understand the basic steps.

1. **Set up your environment:** Choose a programming language (JavaScript or Python), Install required libraries and Set up API access
2. **Implement Core Functionality:** Use one text summarization tool which will accepts user input, sends it to an AI model and returns a summarized response.
3. **Build a front-end or user interface:** Build a simple interface using web technologies, allow users to input text and display results clearly
4. **Deploy Your Application:** Use cloud platforms for hosting, secure your API keys and ensure performance and Scalability.

INTEGRATING AI INTO EXISTING SYSTEMS

Most organizations already have existing systems. AI can be integrated without rebuilding everything.

1. **Microservice Approach:** Create a separate AI service, connect it to existing applications and Add features like summarization or recommendations

2. **Event-Driven Architecture:** Trigger AI actions based on events.

   Example: new ticket → AI summarizes and assigns priority

3. **Data Privacy and Security:** Encrypt sensitive information before sending it to a third-party API, Filter out PII or proprietary snippets when possible, Audit prompts and responses to ensure compliance with regulations.

4. **Performance Considerations:** Cache repeated queries to reduce latency and cost. Batch non-urgent tasks and Monitor costs and response times.

By adding an AI layer instead of rewriting core services, you minimize risk and can roll out new features incrementally.

THE FUTURE OF SOFTWARE DEVELOPMENT WITH AI

AI's impact on development is only beginning. Here's what's on the horizon:

- **Low-Code and No-Code Platforms:** Build applications with minimal coding. AI will generate entire modules based on business requirements, making app building accessible to non-developers.

- **Automated Code Reviews and Security Scans:** AI identifies bugs and suggests improvements. Models will flag vulnerabilities, enforce style standards, and suggest architectural improvements in real time.
- **Multi-Modal Development:** Convert designs or sketches into working code. Imagine sketching a UI on paper and having AI generate the corresponding HTML/CSS and JavaScript interactions.
- **AI-Assisted Architecture Design:** Routine coding tasks will be delegated to AI, while humans focus on designing user experiences, defining requirements, and ensuring ethical use.

To stay relevant:

1. Deepen your understanding of AI like concepts data ethics, prompt engineering, model limitations.
2. Embrace continuous learning experiment with new models, libraries, and platforms.
3. Cultivate soft skills communication, domain expertise, and system design will become increasingly valuable.

CONCLUSION

Artificial Intelligence is transforming software development from a manual process into a collaborative experience. It enables developers to Write code faster, automate repetitive tasks, build smarter applications and focus on innovation and creativity.

In this chapter, you learned how to:

- Use AI-assisted coding tools
- Automate workflows with AI APIs
- Build your first AI-powered application
- Integrate AI into existing systems
- Prepare for the future of development

The most important takeaway is this: **AI is not replacing developers it is empowering them to achieve more.**

Start small:

- Use AI to assist with coding
- Automate simple tasks
- Build a basic AI-powered tool

As you gain confidence, you can explore more advanced applications. The future of software development is not just human-driven or AI-driven it is a collaboration between both.

CHAPTER 15

AI FOR CREATIVE PROFESSIONALS

INTRODUCTION

Creativity has always been considered a uniquely human strength driven by imagination, emotion, and personal expression. Artificial Intelligence is transforming the creative process in ways that were once unimaginable.

Imagine having:

- A co-writer who helps you brainstorm ideas instantly
- A designer who creates visuals from simple descriptions
- A video editor who produces content in minutes

AI is not replacing creativity it is **enhancing it.**

For writers, designers, artists, marketers, and content creators, AI acts as a powerful assistant that accelerates workflows, sparks inspiration, and removes creative blocks.

In this chapter, you will learn how AI can support:

- Writing and storytelling
- Image and visual content creation
- Video and audio production
- Design and branding
- Maintaining authenticity while using AI

By the end of this chapter, you will understand how to use AI as a creative partner—one that amplifies your ideas without replacing your voice.

WRITING, STORYTELLING, AND CONTENT CREATION WITH AI

Imagine having an ever-ready co-writer who never tires, never blanks on ideas, and can spin up article outlines in seconds. That's AI in your writing toolkit. Tools like ChatGPT, Jasper, and Copy.ai excel at brainstorming blog topics, drafting email campaigns, and even helping you overcome writer's block.

Start by feeding an AI a clear prompt: "Write an engaging introduction for a blog about sustainable travel." The AI will generate several options. You can pick your favorite, mix and match sentences, or use them as springboards for your own voice. Use AI to craft outlines sections, bullet points, key statistics then flesh them out with your personal insights, anecdotes, and expertise. The result? You slash hours off the writing process without losing your unique perspective.

Best Practices for Writers:

- Refine your prompts. Be specific about tone, length, and audience.
- Always review and edit. AI drafts can be polished but may contain inaccuracies.
- Inject anecdotes, case studies, or observations that AI can't replicate.
- Use AI repeatedly in iterations each draft becomes closer to your vision.

IMAGE GENERATION: DALL·E, MIDJOURNEY, NANOBANANA AND STABLE DIFFUSION

AI image generation tools allow you to create visuals using simple text descriptions. DALL·E, Midjourney, Nanobanana, Canva and Stable Diffusion lead the pack. You describe the scene "a futuristic city skyline at sunset, watercolor style" and in moments you have several renderings to choose from.

Here's how to get the most out of these tools:

1. Start simple. Test short prompts, then add details: color palettes, lighting, mood.
2. Iterate. Save the versions you like, tweak prompts, and refine until you're amazed.
3. Combine outputs. Use photo editors to layer AI images, adjust composition, or mask elements.

Example: An indie game developer needed concept art for a mystical forest. By iterating prompts in Midjourney "lush enchanted forest, bioluminescent plants, misty ambiance "they quickly generated dozens of mood-board images, speeding pre-production from weeks to days.

VIDEO AND AUDIO CREATION WITH AI TOOLS

AI is also revolutionizing video and audio production. Tasks that once required specialized tools and skills can now be simplified.

AI tools can convert scripts into videos, generate voiceovers and create avatars and presentations. AI produce professional-quality videos without advanced editing skills. Add transitions and effects automatically

Gone are the days of complex video editing suites and long rendering times. Tools like Pictory, Runway ML, and Synthesia, Higgsfield, Haygen, Nanobanana, Kling let you storyboard, generate scenes, and even create AI avatars that speak your script. Simply upload a text script or raw footage and let AI handle scene transitions, voiceovers, or background music.

AI can help with Audio and Music Creation, Podcast editing and transcription, Voice generation and narration, Music composition and background sound.

For podcasters and musicians, platforms such as Descript, AIVA, and Podcast.ai offer:

Automated transcription and editing, AI-generated background music or soundscapes and Voice cloning for additional narration

Imagine promoting a new product: you paste your promotional script into Synthesia, choose an AI presenter, and within minutes have a polished video. No camera crew needed. Or you craft a 30-second jingle in AIVA, customizing tempo and instrumentation with a few clicks.

AI IN DESIGN: CANVA AI, ADOBE FIREFLY, AND MORE

Designers and marketers can now harness AI to generate color palettes, layout suggestions, and image backgrounds. Canva AI's Magic Resize automatically adapts a Facebook post into an Instagram story or Twitter banner. Adobe Firefly can erase backgrounds, generate textures, or suggest font pairings that align with your brand identity.

Use cases:

- **Social media manager:** batch-produce branded graphics using templates enhanced by AI.
- **Event planner:** design flyers and posters with on-brand visuals in minutes.
- **Small business owner:** craft professional marketing materials without hiring a designer.

Remember, AI is a collaborator. Accept its suggestions, then tweak spacing, replace icons, or adjust contrast to suit your vision. This partnership can transform a one-hour design task into a ten-minute sprint.

STAYING AUTHENTIC WHILE LEVERAGING AI CREATIVITY

With so much automation, it is important to maintain your unique voice and identity. But your unique voice, perspective, and experiences are what differentiate your work. Here's how to maintain authenticity:

1. Treat AI as a starting point. Use its output like rough clay you shape, refine, and add texture.

2. Incorporate your personal stories, opinions, or stylistic quirks that AI can't mimic.
3. Credit AI when appropriate especially in collaborative spaces or published works.
4. Set boundaries. Decide what tasks you'll delegate to AI and which you'll handle manually.

Example: A novelist used ChatGPT to explore alternate plot twists. She then merged her favorite ideas with her characters' established arcs, ensuring the final story felt 100 percent hers.

CONCLUSION

Artificial Intelligence is redefining creativity by making powerful tools accessible to everyone. AI offers creative professionals unprecedented speed, flexibility, and inspiration. Whether you're drafting blog posts, generating concept art, editing videos, or designing social media assets, these tools amplify your talent rather than replace it. Embrace experimentation: tweak prompts, combine outputs, and always layer in your personal touch. By balancing AI's efficiency with your human insight, you'll transform not just your workflow, but your entire creative practice and emerge more relevant and innovative than ever.

The most important takeaway is this: **AI does not replace creativity, it amplifies it.**

As you grow more comfortable, you will discover new ways to integrate AI into your creative process. The future of creativity is not human versus AI it is human creativity enhanced by AI. And with the right approach, you can create faster, smarter, and more innovatively than ever before.

PART 5

RESPONSIBLE AI-ETHICS, SAFETY & THE FUTURE

"With great power comes great responsibility"

CHAPTER 16

THE ETHICS OF AI

INTRODUCTION

Artificial Intelligence is one of the most powerful technologies shaping our world today. It can recommend what we watch, decide which resumes get shortlisted, assist doctors in diagnosing diseases, and even influence financial decisions. But with this power comes an important question: **Can we trust AI to make fair, safe, and responsible decisions?**

Behind every intelligent system are human choices what data is used, how models are designed, and where they are applied. These choices directly impact people's lives. This is why **AI ethics** is not just a technical topic it is a human responsibility.

In this chapter, you will explore:

- How bias enters AI systems and how to identify it
- Why data privacy matters more than ever
- The risks of deepfakes and misinformation
- Who is responsible when AI systems fail
- How to build your own ethical framework for using AI

By the end, you will have a clearer understanding of how to use AI responsibly and thoughtfully in both personal and professional settings.

BIAS IN AI: UNDERSTANDING THE HIDDEN PROBLEM

Imagine you apply for a job and never hear back. Later you discover the AI resume screener flagged your application unfairly. This scenario isn't fiction bias in AI can silently shape life-changing decisions. At its core, AI bias arises when a system learns from historical data that reflects existing prejudices or unbalanced representation. If a facial-recognition model is trained primarily on lighter skin tones, it struggles to accurately identify darker-skinned faces. If a loan-approval algorithm sees more approved applications from one neighborhood, it may penalize applicants from another.

How do you spot bias? Look for patterns in decisions that correlate with race, gender, age, or geography. If you notice a certain group consistently getting worse outcomes from higher interest rates to lower job interview callbacks that's a red flag. Ask questions: What data was used to train this model? Is the data diverse and representative? Were fairness checks performed? Many organizations now perform "bias audits," testing AI outputs across diverse groups. As a curious learner or working professional, you can start by running simple experiments. Test the system by changing small inputs (such as names or locations) and compare results across different demographics. Transparency from developers and third-party auditing tools can help reveal hidden biases before they do real harm.

Unchecked bias can lead to Unfair hiring decisions, Discrimination in financial services and Unequal access to opportunities. Recognizing bias is the first step toward building fairer systems.

PRIVACY CONCERNS AND YOUR DATA

Every click, swipe, and voice command adds to an ever-growing mountain of personal data. AI systems thrive on this information, using your search history to recommend products, your health records to predict disease risk, or your location data to optimize traffic flows. While these applications can be beneficial, they also raise serious privacy concerns. Who owns your data? How long is it stored? Is it shared with third parties?

Regulations like Europe's GDPR and California's CCPA give individuals more control rights to access, correct, or delete personal data. But many apps request blanket permissions, bundling consent for data sharing in dense privacy policies few read. To protect yourself, take simple steps: review app permissions on your phone, disable tracking where possible, and use privacy-focused browsers or VPNs. When you sign up for a new service, look for clear statements about data usage and ask whether you can opt out of secondary sharing. Responsible organizations will offer transparency dashboards showing what they collect and why.

You can take simple steps to safeguard your privacy by reviewing app permissions regularly, disabling unnecessary tracking, use secure and privacy-focused tools, read privacy policies (at least the key sections).

Even anonymized data can sometimes be re-identified. This is why organizations must adopt **privacy-by-design principles**, ensuring that user data is protected from the start not as an afterthought.

DEEPFAKES, MISINFORMATION, AND AI MISUSE

One of the most concerning uses of AI is the creation of misleading or false content. Deepfakes are AI-generated media that can Alter faces in videos, Clone voices and create realistic but fake content. This makes it possible to Spread false information, Damage reputations and manipulate public opinion.

Imagine seeing a video of a world leader announcing a false policy, or reading an AI-crafted social media post designed to sway your opinion on election day. These manipulations are no longer the stuff of spy novels; they're emerging threats accessible to anyone with a laptop.

Deepfake technology combines techniques like generative adversarial networks (GANs) with readily available open-source tools, making it possible to swap faces or voices in realistic ways. Misinformation campaigns can deploy these tools to discredit individuals, amplify fear, or stoke division. To protect yourself, develop a healthy skepticism: verify sources, look for corroborating evidence from reputable outlets, and use reverse-image searches to trace media origins. Platforms and fact-checking organizations are building AI defenses watermarking authentic content, flagging suspicious edits, and training detection algorithms. As a user, you can support these efforts by reporting questionable posts and educating your network about common signs of manipulation, such as inconsistent lighting, unnatural facial expressions, or mismatched audio lip sync. Cross-check news and media. Be cautious before sharing content.

WHO IS RESPONSIBLE WHEN AI GOES WRONG?

If an autonomous vehicle causes an accident, who is at fault the carmaker, the software developer, the car owner, or the AI itself? Traditional liability frameworks struggle to keep up with AI's complexity. Programmers write code, data scientists curate datasets, and end users choose how to deploy AI systems. Each party shares some responsibility, but clear lines can blur.

Regulators are exploring new models: strict liability for manufacturers of high-risk AI systems, mandatory insurance schemes, or AI "black box" transparency rules requiring logs of decision processes. In 2021, the EU proposed an AI Act categorizing systems by risk level and imposing duties accordingly. High-risk systems such as those in healthcare, transportation, or law enforcement would face stringent testing and documentation requirements. Meanwhile, courts in different countries are grappling with lawsuits that challenge existing notions of negligence and product liability.

For professionals working with or deploying AI, proactive steps matter. Maintain thorough documentation of development choices, testing protocols, and performance metrics. Implement clear audit trails so you can trace a decision back to its data and code. When selecting third-party AI tools, insist on vendor guarantees and insurance coverage for errors. By embedding accountability measures into every phase from design to deployment, you help ensure that responsibility doesn't vanish into a black box. Governments and organizations are working on Regulations for high-risk AI systems, Transparency requirements, Audit and compliance standards.

BUILDING A PERSONAL ETHICAL FRAMEWORK FOR AI USE

Ethical AI isn't just a corporate buzzword it's a personal compass guiding your everyday decisions. Whether you're a manager choosing an AI vendor, a developer writing code, or an end user deciding which apps to install, a clear framework helps you navigate moral gray areas. Here's a simple five-step guide:

1. Define your values. What matters most to your fairness, transparency, privacy, safety? Write down two or three core principles that will steer your AI choices.

2. Ask critical questions. Before adopting an AI tool, probe its origins: Who built it? What data was used? How was it tested? What known limitations exist? Treat vendors like partners, not black-box suppliers.
3. Seek diverse perspectives. Invite colleagues or peers with different backgrounds to review your AI projects. Diversity in viewpoints helps uncover blind spots that echo chambers often miss.
4. Document and reflect. Keep a brief ethical impact log: note potential risks, mitigation plans, and any concerns raised during development or deployment. Revisit this log periodically as the project evolves.
5. Commit to ongoing learning. AI ethics is a dynamic field. New research on fairness metrics, privacy-preserving techniques, and regulatory changes emerge regularly. Subscribe to industry newsletters, join ethics working groups, or participate in online forums to stay informed.

By turning these steps into habits, you transform abstract principles into everyday practice. You become not only a consumer of AI but a steward of its responsible use.

CONCLUSION

Artificial Intelligence offers incredible opportunities but it also comes with serious responsibilities.

In this chapter, you explored:

- The causes and impact of bias in AI
- The importance of protecting personal data
- The risks of deepfakes and misinformation
- The challenge of accountability
- How to build your own ethical framework

The most important takeaway is this: **AI is only as responsible as the people who design and use it.**

As you continue your journey:

- Stay aware of ethical challenges
- Make informed decisions
- Use AI thoughtfully and responsibly

The future of AI is not just about innovation it is about building systems that are fair, transparent, and trustworthy and the responsibility belongs to all of us.

CHAPTER 17

AI SAFETY–WHAT THE EXPERTS ARE SAYING

INTRODUCTION

Artificial Intelligence is advancing at an incredible pace. From helping us write content to assisting in healthcare and business decisions, AI is becoming deeply integrated into our daily lives. But with this rapid progress comes an important and often uncomfortable question:

Is AI safe and how do we ensure it remains beneficial for humanity?

This question is not just being asked by researchers. It is being debated by scientists, policymakers, and global organizations.

In this chapter, you will explore how leading AI companies are building safety into their systems, the challenges faced by organizations like OpenAI and Anthropic, how governments around the world are responding, the ongoing debate about long-term AI risks, and practical principles for responsible AI development.

By the end of this chapter, you will gain a balanced understanding of AI safety what experts agree on, where opinions differ, and what it means for the future.

WHY SAFETY IS BUILT INTO MODERN AI SYSTEMS

One of the most important shifts in AI development today is simple yet powerful: **Safety is no longer optional it is essential.**

When Anthropic developed its AI system Claude, it made a deliberate decision to place safety at the very core of the system rather than treating it as an afterthought. This approach, known as constitutional AI, embeds guiding principles directly into the model's behavior. These principles include being helpful, honest, and aligned with user intent while actively avoiding harmful or dangerous outputs.

A helpful way to understand this approach is to think of it as teaching a child with a strong moral foundation. Every time the AI generates a response, it evaluates that response against its internal rules and revises it if necessary. This creates a continuous cycle of generation, evaluation, and improvement, ensuring that safety is not a one-time filter but an ongoing process embedded in every interaction.

WHY ANTHROPIC BUILT CLAUDE WITH SAFETY AT ITS CORE

When Anthropic set out to create its AI assistant Claude, the team decided not to treat safety as an afterthought or a tacked-on feature but as the very foundation of the system. Inspired by a deep belief that advanced AI should benefit humanity without causing harm, Anthropic's researchers developed what they call a "constitutional AI" approach. They wrote an explicit set of guiding principles clarity, honesty, respect for user intent, avoidance of harmful advice and built Claude's learning algorithms to follow them at every step.

Imagine teaching a child with a code of conduct that says "always tell the truth," "respect others," and "never offer dangerous guidance." Every time that child learns from new experiences, you remind them of these rules, correct them when they forget, and reinforce the positive behaviors. That's essentially how Anthropic trains Claude. The model generates a response, checks it against its internal constitution, and if anything violates the principles, it revises or rejects the answer. This iterative process of generation, critique, and refinement make safety an ongoing conversation inside the AI, not a final checkbox.

OPENAI'S SAFETY RESEARCH AND CHALLENGES

OpenAI took a multi-pronged approach to safety as it scaled from GPT-2 to GPT-4. Researchers introduced Reinforcement Learning from Human Feedback (RLHF), where human evaluators rank machine-generated outputs, teaching the model to prefer correct, helpful, and harmless answers. They set up red-team exercises security experts and language hackers try to trick or jailbreak the system to expose weaknesses before the public ever interacts with it.

Challenges remained, though. Scaling laws that make models more capable also enable new, unforeseen behaviors. A bigger model that writes poetry might suddenly draft convincing phishing emails or develop persistent biases. OpenAI has admitted that every new release carries unknown risks. Balancing openness with public demos, API access, community research and caution delaying features until safety nets are in place is a tightrope walk. OpenAI's Charter emphasizes long-term safety research and cooperation with external experts to share lessons and avoid duplicating dangerous mistakes.

GOVERNMENT REGULATIONS AND AI POLICY WORLDWIDE

As private labs race ahead, governments are drafting rules. In the United States, the White House issued an Executive Order on AI safety, encouraging federal agencies to develop guidelines on secure design, transparency, and risk assessment. The National Institute of Standards and Technology (NIST) is working on an AI risk management framework for public comment.

Across the Atlantic, the European Union's AI Act categorizes AI applications by risk level, banning certain high-risk uses such as predictive policing and enforcing strict requirements on transparency, human oversight, and data governance. In China, regulators have published draft rules for recommendation algorithms, requiring clear labeling of synthetic content and limiting addictive design patterns.

International bodies like UNESCO and the OECD are proposing global principles fairness, accountability, human rights, sustainability while the United Nations convenes experts to discuss existential threats. The patchwork of guidelines reflects different cultural and political priorities, but the message is the same: left unchecked, advanced AI could pose serious risks to privacy, fairness, security, and even global stability.

THE BIG DEBATE: SHOULD WE BE WORRIED ABOUT AI?

Experts do not all agree on the level of risk posed by AI, and this has led to an ongoing global debate.

Some researchers focus on long-term risks. Philosopher Nick Bostrom has argued that highly advanced AI systems could become difficult to control if they are not properly aligned with human values. A well-known thought experiment, often referred to as the "paperclip problem," illustrates how an AI pursuing a simple goal without constraints could unintentionally cause harm by ignoring broader human needs.

On the other hand, experts such as Yann LeCun and Andrew Ng believe that the focus should remain on immediate challenges. These include issues like bias, misinformation, job displacement, and cybersecurity. They argue that current AI systems are powerful tools but do not possess independent intent or autonomy.

A balanced perspective is offered by Stuart Russell, who suggests designing AI systems that remain uncertain about human preferences and actively seek clarification when needed. This approach emphasizes keeping humans in control and ensuring that AI systems operate as collaborative tools rather than independent decision-makers.

WHAT RESPONSIBLE AI DEVELOPMENT LOOKS LIKE

Despite differing opinions on long-term risks, experts broadly agree on several best practices for responsible AI development.

First, building diverse and multidisciplinary teams is essential. AI development should not be limited to engineers alone. Including ethicists, legal experts, and domain specialists helps identify potential risks and biases from multiple perspectives.

Second, transparency plays a critical role. Organizations must clearly document how their AI systems are built, including the data used for training, known limitations, and steps taken to mitigate risks. This openness builds trust and allows others to evaluate the system more effectively.

Third, rigorous testing is necessary. Techniques such as adversarial testing and red teaming help uncover weaknesses before systems are deployed in real-world scenarios.

Fourth, human oversight remains crucial, especially in high-impact areas such as healthcare, finance, and legal decision-making. AI should support human judgment not replace it.

Fifth, continuous monitoring is required after deployment. AI systems must be regularly evaluated to detect bias, errors, or unexpected behavior, and updated accordingly.

Finally, engaging with policymakers and the broader public helps ensure that AI development aligns with societal values. Open dialogue encourages accountability and fosters trust.

The Bigger Picture: Safety as a Shared Responsibility

AI safety is not the responsibility of a single group it is a shared responsibility. Developers must design systems thoughtfully, organizations must deploy them responsibly, policymakers must create appropriate regulations, and users must engage with AI critically and responsibly. Every interaction with AI contributes to shaping its impact on society.

CONCLUSION

AI safety is one of the most important conversations of our time.

In this chapter, you explored how leading organizations approach safety, the challenges of building responsible systems, global efforts to regulate AI, the ongoing debate about risks, and practical strategies for ethical development.

The most important takeaway is this: **AI is powerful but it must be guided responsibly.**

As AI continues to evolve, staying informed, thinking critically, and making responsible choices will be essential. The future of AI is not just about technological advancement it is about ensuring that this advancement benefits humanity as a whole and that responsibility belongs to all of us.

CHAPTER 18

THE FUTURE OF AI -WHAT'S COMING NEXT

INTRODUCTION

Artificial Intelligence has already become a part of our everyday lives. From voice assistants that wake us up in the morning to recommendation systems that shape what we watch, read, and buy, AI is quietly influencing how we live and work. Yet, what we see today is only the beginning. The future of AI holds even greater possibilities systems that can reason more deeply, act more independently, and collaborate more closely with humans.

In this chapter, you will explore what lies ahead. You will understand the concept of Artificial General Intelligence, the rise of autonomous AI agents, the impact on jobs and industries, and the skills you need to stay relevant in an AI-driven world.

By the end, you will not only understand where AI is heading but also how to prepare for it.

AGI: ARTIFICIAL GENERAL INTELLIGENCE, HOW CLOSE ARE WE?

Imagine a machine that can learn anything a human can, apply knowledge across different fields, and adapt to entirely new situations without retraining.

This is the vision of **Artificial General Intelligence (AGI)**.

Today's AI systems are highly capable, but they are still specialized. They can perform specific tasks extremely well such as translating languages, recognizing images, or analyzing data but they do not possess general intelligence.

Recent advancements in large-scale models and hybrid systems have brought us closer to this goal. These systems can handle multiple types of data and demonstrate improved reasoning capabilities. However, several major challenges remain.

One of the biggest challenges is common-sense reasoning. Humans effortlessly understand everyday situations, but AI often struggles with basic assumptions. Another challenge is transferring learning the ability to apply knowledge learned in one context to a completely new situation. While AI has improved in this area, it is still limited.

Perhaps the most important challenge is ethical alignment. Ensuring that advanced AI systems behave in ways that are consistent with human values is complex and requires careful design.

Most experts believe that AGI is still years, if not decades, away. However, the rapid pace of progress means that breakthroughs could happen sooner than expected.

AI AGENTS AND AUTONOMOUS SYSTEMS

The future of AI is not just about smarter models it is about more capable systems that can act independently.AI agents are systems that can perceive their environment, make decisions, and take actions. When combined with sensors, robotics, and connectivity, they form autonomous systems.

Today, we already see early examples of this in everyday life. ***Customer service chatbots handle conversations without human intervention.*** Warehouse robots manage inventory and logistics. Self-driving technologies are being developed to transform transportation.

These systems operate through layered architectures. First, perception systems gather data from the environment through cameras, sensors, or audio inputs. This information is then processed by AI models that interpret and understand the data. Next, decision-making systems analyze possible actions and choose the most appropriate one. Finally, actuation systems carry out the action whether it is moving a robot, sending a message, or executing a transaction.

As these systems become more advanced, they will take on more complex responsibilities. They may assist in remote maintenance, support medical procedures, or manage financial operations.

For professionals, the key is not to compete with AI agents but to learn how to collaborate with them effectively.

AI AND THE JOB MARKET -THREAT OR OPPORTUNITY?

One of the most widely discussed topics about AI is its impact on jobs. While it is true that AI will automate certain tasks, history shows that technological advancements also create new opportunities.

Roles at risk

Routine roles such as data entry, basic customer support, and repetitive analysis are more likely to be automated. At the same time, new roles are emerging that focus on working alongside AI.

Emerging opportunities

AI trainers who help improve models, explainability experts who make AI decisions understandable, and ethics specialists who ensure responsible use. Additionally, many roles are becoming hybrid, combining domain expertise with AI skills.

Hybrid roles combining domain expertise with AI tool proficiency like marketing analysts who leverage generative AI, healthcare professionals using diagnostic assistants.

Upskilling for resilience

Embrace lifelong learning. Online courses and bootcamps in AI literacy, data analysis, and human–machine collaboration are more accessible than ever.

Develop soft skills: creative problem solving, emotional intelligence, critical thinking—that machines can't replicate.

Focus on strategic thinking: designing processes, interpreting AI insights, and making value-driven decisions.

AI will reshape job descriptions, but those who adapt will find themselves in higher-value, more creative roles.

INDUSTRIES THAT WILL BE COMPLETELY TRANSFORMED

AI's impact will be felt across every industry, but some sectors are experiencing especially rapid transformation.

Healthcare: AI is enabling early disease detection through predictive analytics, supporting personalized treatment plans based on patient data, and providing virtual health assistants for continuous monitoring. These advancements improve both efficiency and patient outcomes.

Finance: AI is revolutionizing areas such as trading, fraud detection, and wealth management. Systems can analyze vast amounts of data in real time, identify anomalies, and make informed recommendations.

Manufacturing is evolving into smart production environments where machines optimize processes automatically. Predictive maintenance reduces downtime, while customization allows products to be tailored to individual preferences at scale.

Education is becoming more personalized through adaptive learning platforms that adjust to each student's pace and style. AI also supports educators by automating administrative tasks and providing insights into student performance.

Retail and supply chain operations are being enhanced through demand forecasting, autonomous delivery systems, and real-time inventory optimization.

Across all these industries, organizations that embrace AI strategically will gain a significant competitive advantage.

Emerging Roles and Opportunities

As some tasks vanish, new roles will emerge around AI creation, oversight, and integration:

- **AI Trainers and Labelers:** People who curate and label data to teach AI systems how to interpret images, text, or speech accurately.
- **Ethics and Compliance Specialists:** Professionals addressing bias, privacy, and regulatory concerns to ensure responsible AI deployment.
- **AI Integration Managers:** Employees who coordinate between technology teams and business units, aligning AI tools with organizational goals.
- **Human–Machine Interaction Designers:** Experts crafting intuitive interfaces and workflows so humans and AI systems collaborate smoothly.

Shifting Skill Demands

The future workforce will require:

- **Digital Literacy:** Comfort with AI tools and the ability to evaluate their outputs.
- **Data Fluency:** Interpreting AI-generated insights and making informed decisions.
- **Adaptability:** Willingness to learn new platforms and pivot as tools evolve.
- **Complex Communication:** Translating technical results into clear business recommendations.

Organizations will seek candidates who blend technical understanding with problem-solving and interpersonal skills.

Industry Case Studies

- **Healthcare:** AI-driven imaging analysis can spot anomalies in X-rays faster than humans, yet doctors remain essential for diagnosis, patient communication, and treatment planning.
- **Finance:** Algorithmic trading and risk modeling handle voluminous data, but human judgment governs strategy, regulation, and client relationships.

- **Creative Fields:** AI tools can generate music, art, or marketing copy, yet human creators set the vision, tone, and emotional nuance.

What Will Remain

Despite rapid advancements in AI, certain human qualities will remain irreplaceable.

Human Creativity and Imagination

Creativity and imagination are uniquely human strengths. While AI can generate content based on patterns, it lacks true originality and lived experience. Breakthrough ideas and innovations will continue to come from human insight.

Emotional Intelligence and Empathy

Understanding emotions, building relationship, and motivating teams are inherently human capabilities. Careers in counseling, leadership, teaching, and negotiation rely on genuine empathy and trust. AI can simulate empathy through scripted responses but cannot authentically relate to another person's emotional journey.

Ethical Judgment and Moral Responsibility

AI makes decisions based on data and programmed objectives, but it cannot hold moral values or understand societal implications independently.

Humans must guide AI with ethical frameworks, decide acceptable trade-offs, and remain accountable for errors or unintended consequences.

Complex Problem-Solving and Strategic Vision

Global challenges from climate change to economic inequality require holistic approaches that blend technical knowledge, ethical considerations, and political acumen. While AI can model scenarios or optimize processes, humans connect dots across disciplines to craft long-term strategies.

HOW TO FUTURE-PROOF YOUR CAREER WITH AI

Preparing for the future does not require becoming an AI expert overnight. Instead, it involves taking practical and consistent steps.

Start by building awareness. Explore beginner-friendly resources, experiment with AI tools, and understand their capabilities and limitations. This foundational knowledge will help you navigate the evolving landscape.

Next, develop complementary skills. Focus on critical thinking, creativity, and problem-solving. These skills enhance your ability to work effectively with AI.

Engage in cross-functional collaboration. Participate in projects that involve AI and learn how to bridge the gap between technical teams and business needs.

Adopt an ethical mindset. Understand the importance of responsible AI use and advocate for transparency and fairness in your work.

Finally, commit to continuous learning. Stay updated with new developments, join communities, and learn from real-world applications.

By taking these steps, you position yourself not just to adapt but to lead in an AI-driven world.

CONCLUSION

The future of AI is both exciting and uncertain.

While the idea of Artificial General Intelligence may still be on the horizon, the technologies being developed today are already transforming industries, careers, and everyday experiences.

The most important perspective to adopt is this: **AI is not something happening to you, it is something you can actively engage with.**

By understanding where AI is heading, developing the right skills, and embracing a mindset of continuous learning, you can turn uncertainty into opportunity.

The future will not belong to those who resist change but to those who learn, adapt, and collaborate with AI.

And that future starts now.

PART 6

YOUR AI JOURNEY-BECOMING AN EXPERT

"You started as Beginner. Now it's time to own your AI future"

CHAPTER 19

YOUR PERSONAL AI ACTION PLAN

INTRODUCTION

Imagine having a personal digital assistant that works 24/7, never tires, learns from your preferences, and helps you to complete tasks faster than ever before. That is the real promise of Artificial Intelligence not just as a concept, but as a practical tool you can use every day. However, the real value of AI does not come from simply knowing about it. It comes from **using it consistently and strategically.**

Whether you are a beginner exploring AI for the first time or a professional looking to stay ahead, this chapter will help you turn knowledge into action. You will learn how to choose the right tools, decide between free and paid options, build daily habits, and follow a structured 30-day plan to master AI in a practical way.

By the end of this chapter, you will have a clear and personalized roadmap to integrate AI into your daily life and work.

CHOOSING THE RIGHT AI TOOLS FOR YOUR GOALS

Before you grab every shiny AI app you see, pause and ask: "What problem do I want to solve?" Here's how to align tools with goals:

1. **Identify Your Core Tasks**
    - **Writing and brainstorming:** drafting emails, blog posts, proposals
    - **Data analysis and insights:** crunching spreadsheets, generating charts
    - **Creative design and visuals:** generating images, editing videos
    - **Coding and automation:** writing scripts, debugging, automating workflows
    - **Communication and research:** summarizing articles, translating, answering questions
2. **Match Features to Needs**
    - **Natural-language generation:** ChatGPT, Jasper, Rytr

- **Code assistance:** GitHub Copilot, Tabnine
- **Visual content:** Canva's AI tools, Midjourney, Adobe Firefly
- **Data analysis:** OpenAI functions, Google Sheets AI tools, Tableau AI
- **Multimodal assistants:** Bard (text + images), Claude (reasoning focus)

3. **Evaluate Learning Curve and Integrations**
   - **Ease of use:** drag-and-drop interfaces vs. API configuration
   - **Platform compatibility:** desktop web, mobile apps, browser extensions
   - **Ecosystem fit:** does it work with your existing tools (Slack, Notion, Excel)?
   - **Community and support:** tutorials, user forums, template libraries

Example: If you're a marketing professional drafting copy, start with ChatGPT's templates. If you need quick social-media graphics, test Canva's AI features. Jot down your top three priorities, then sample two to three tools in each category.

FREE VS. PAID AI TOOLS: WHAT'S WORTH IT?

As you explore, you'll notice many AI tools come in free and premium tiers. Here's how to decide when to upgrade:

1. **Free Tools: Great for Exploration**

   Free tools are an excellent starting point. They allow you to experiment without any financial commitment and help you understand the value of AI in your workflow. However, they often come with limitations such as usage restrictions, slower performance, or limited features.

   Examples: ChatGPT's free tier, Google Bard, Hugging Face demo space, Stable Diffusion community models

2. **Paid Tools: Investing in Reliability and Power**

   Paid tools, on the other hand, offer more reliability and advanced capabilities. They typically provide faster responses, higher usage limits, and access to more powerful models. For professionals who rely on AI regularly, these benefits can significantly improve productivity.

   Examples: ChatGPT Plus (faster GPT-4 access), Adobe Firefly premium, Copilot for Business, enterprise API plans

3. **When to Upgrade**

   The decision to upgrade should be based on your needs. If you find yourself frequently hitting limits, requiring faster performance, or needing advanced features for professional work, it may be worth investing in a paid plan.

   Tip: A practical strategy is to begin with free tools, validate their usefulness, and upgrade only when necessary. This ensures that you are making a value-driven decision.

BUILDING DAILY AI HABITS FOR MAXIMUM PRODUCTIVITY

Having access to AI tools is only the first step. The real transformation happens when you build consistent habits around their use.

Start your day with a short AI check-in. Spend a few minutes experimenting with prompts or refining outputs from previous work. This helps you stay engaged and continuously improve your skills.

As you discover prompts that work well, create a personal prompt library. Store them in a simple tool like a note-taking app and organize them by purpose. Over time, this becomes a valuable resource that saves time and improves consistency.

Integrate AI into your existing workflow rather than treating it as a separate activity. For example, you can draft emails using AI, summarize articles while browsing, or automate repetitive tasks in spreadsheets. The goal is to make AI a natural part of your daily routine.

It is also helpful to set aside dedicated time for experimentation. Trying new tools or features regularly helps you stay updated and discover new ways to improve your workflow.

Finally, take time to reflect on your progress. At the end of each week, evaluate what worked well and what did not. Focus on the habits that deliver the most value and refine your approach.

YOUR 30-DAY AI MASTERY ACTION PLAN

A structured plan keeps momentum high. Here's a week-by-week roadmap you can adapt to your schedule:

Week 1: Exploration and Familiarization

- **Day 1–2:** Define your top three tasks (writing, data, design)
- **Day 3–4:** Sign up for two free AI tools in each category

- **Day 5–7:** Complete official tutorials or community walkthroughs

Week 2: Integration into Daily Workflow

- **Day 8–10:** Pick one routine task (email, meeting notes, report summary) and fully AI-assist it
- **Day 11–12:** Build a prompt library; categorize and test saved prompts
- **Day 13–14:** Share early wins with a peer or mentor for feedback

Week 3: Skill Building and Experimentation

- **Day 15–17:** Subscribe to one paid tier if needed; explore advanced features (longer context, image inputs)
- **Day 18–20:** Try an AI tool outside your comfort zone (e.g., code generation, visual design)
- **Day 21:** Host an "AI jam session" brainstorm with colleagues or friends using your favorite tool

Week 4: Reflection, Refinement, and Project

- **Day 22–24:** Review usage data identify your most and least used tools

- **Day 25–27:** Refine your favorite prompts; drop or replace tools that underperformed
- **Day 28–30:** Build a capstone mini-project (e.g., a report, a marketing campaign outline, a small web app) using your toolkit; document your process and results

At Day 30, you'll have a clear sense of which AI tools and habits serve you best. Celebrate your progress and plan next steps whether deepening your skills or exploring new AI frontiers.

CONCLUSION

Artificial Intelligence is one of the most powerful tools available today but its value depends on how you use it.

In this chapter, you learned how to:

- Choose the right AI tools based on your goals
- Decide between free and paid options
- Build daily habits that improve productivity
- Follow a structured 30-day plan to master AI

The most important takeaway is this:

You do not need to master AI all at once you need to start using it consistently.

Begin with a single tool. Write your first prompt. Experiment, learn, and refine.

As you continue, AI will evolve from a tool into a trusted partner one that helps you work smarter, learn faster, and achieve more.

Your AI journey does not start tomorrow.

It starts now.

CHAPTER 20
STAYING CURRENT IN A FAST-MOVING FIELD

INTRODUCTION

Artificial Intelligence is evolving at an extraordinary pace. New tools, research breakthroughs, and real-world applications are emerging almost every day. For many learners and professionals, it can feel overwhelming—like trying to keep up with a constantly moving target.

But staying current in AI is not about knowing everything. It is about building smart habits that help you stay informed, adapt quickly, and continue growing over time.

Whether you are a beginner, a curious learner, or a working professional, this chapter will guide you on how to stay updated without burnout. You will learn how to follow the right sources, evaluate new tools effectively, build a strong network, and develop lifelong learning strategies.

By the end of this chapter, you will have a clear system to stay relevant in one of the fastest-moving fields in the world.

BEST NEWSLETTERS, PODCASTS, AND COMMUNITIES FOR AI

In a field as dynamic as AI, information is everywhere but not all of it is useful.

Instead of trying to consume everything, focus on **curated and high-quality sources.** Newsletters, podcasts, and online communities play a key role in filtering out noise and delivering valuable insights.

1. **Newsletters**
    - **The Batch (Andrew Ng's newsletter):** Bite-sized summaries of top research, industry updates, and applied AI projects. Its conversational style makes complex ideas digestible.
    - **Import AI (Jack Clark):** In-depth analysis of AI policy, ethics, and cutting-edge research, ideal for those who want more context around technical advances.

- **AI Weekly:** A quick roundup of news, tutorials, and open-source releases, great for beginners seeking a broad overview.
- **Tip:** Subscribe to two or three, then prune based on which you actually read each week. Quality over quantity beats inbox overload.

2. **Podcasts**
   - **Lex Fridman Podcast:** Long-form interviews with AI researchers, entrepreneurs, and thinkers. Perfect for commutes or workouts when you can immerse yourself in deep conversations.
   - **TWIML AI Podcast (This Week in Machine Learning & AI):** Shorter episodes highlighting new tools, interviews with practitioners, and case studies of real-world applications.
   - **Data Skeptic:** Explores AI concepts, statistical techniques, and skepticism around data claims, delivered in accessible, story-driven segments.
   - **Tip:** Use podcast playlists or speed controls to fit episodes into your workflow. Jot down one insight per episode to reinforce memory.
3. **Online Communities**
   - **Reddit (r/Machine Learning):** Peer support for questions, code reviews, and resource

recommendations. Lurk first; then start by upvoting quality content to build credibility.

- **Discord & Slack Groups:** Many frameworks (TensorFlow, PyTorch) and specialized topics (AI ethics, computer vision) have active channels where you can ask questions and share projects.
- **LinkedIn & Meetup:** Local AI meetups, hackathons, and professional groups help you connect face-to-face, build accountability buddies, and find collaborators.
- **Tip:** Contribute before you ask. Share your own mini-projects, post your takeaways from a paper, or offer to help newcomers. Engagement breeds deeper learning and reputation.

HOW TO EVALUATE NEW AI TOOLS AS THEY LAUNCH

Every week seems to bring a new AI chatbot, image generator, or analytics platform promising revolutionary results. Here's a simple framework to cut through the hype:

1. **Clarify Your Objective**

   Ask: What problem am I solving? If you need to automate customer support, test chatbots; if you're generating creative assets, explore image- or text-generation tools. Avoid tool-first mindsets start with the need.

2. **Check Credibility and Maturity**

   Who's behind it? Established research labs or scrappy startups? Review technical documentation and any peer-reviewed papers. Search for user testimonials or case studies.

   Beta vs. Production: Beta releases are great for experimentation but may lack stability or security. Gauge whether you need a bleeding-edge prototype or a reliable solution for mission-critical tasks.

3. **Hands-On Trial**

   Sandbox environment: Create a test account or use a free tier to experiment. Feed representative inputs and measure outputs against benchmarks or your own quality criteria.

   Performance Metrics: For a language model, evaluate fluency, factual accuracy, and bias. For a computer vision API, measure precision, recall, and latency. Gather both quantitative and qualitative feedback.

4. **Integration and Workflow Fit**

   APIs & SDKs: Does it plug into your existing codebases or platforms? Are there wrappers for your preferred language?

User Experience: Is the interface intuitive? How steep is the learning curve for nontechnical stakeholders?

5. **Cost–Benefit Analysis**

   Pricing Models: Subscription, pay-per-use, enterprise license. Project your monthly or annual spend at different usage levels.

   ROI Estimation: Estimate time saved, additional revenue enabled, or brand value gained. Even approximate numbers help justify investment to yourself or your organization.

Real-World Example: When the latest text-to-speech tool launched, a marketing team needed lifelike voiceovers for tutorial videos. They ran samples through several tools, compared voice naturalness and pronunciation of industry jargon, and measured cost per minute of audio. Armed with data, they chose the tool that balanced quality and budget—and negotiated an enterprise discount.

BUILDING A NETWORK OF AI-FORWARD PEERS

No matter how sharp you are, you accelerate your growth when you surround yourself with people who push you, share insights, and open doors. Here's how to cultivate that circle:

1. **Attend Events Regularly**

   Conferences (e.g., NeurIPS, AI Summit): Even virtual attendance gives you access to cutting-edge talks and networking lounges.

   Local Meetups & Hackathons: Smaller gatherings can be less intimidating and more action-oriented. Join or volunteer to help organize to deepen your ties.

2. **Leverage Social Media Strategically**

   Twitter/X: Follow leading researchers, tool developers, and thought leaders. Engage by asking thoughtful questions or sharing mini-threads on your experiments.

   LinkedIn: Post project updates, articles you find fascinating, or short lessons learned. Tag collaborators to amplify reach.

3. **Find or Become a Mentor**

   Mentor Up and Down: Seek guidance from someone ahead of you while mentoring novices. Teaching cements your learning, and you'll gain fresh perspectives from beginners' questions.

4. **Collaborate on Side Projects**

   Open-Source Contributions: Fix bugs, add features, or improve documentation. You'll work alongside maintainers and power users.

Team Up for Mini Research: Reproduce a recent paper, build a toy demo, or enter a Kaggle competition together. Shared challenges forge lasting bonds.

5. **Keep the Relationship Alive**

   One-on-One Check-Ins: A monthly or quarterly chat over coffee or video call keeps you updated on each other's progress.

   Knowledge-Sharing Sessions: Host a lunchtime "lightning talk" where peers present a new tool or paper in ten minutes followed by discussion.

CONTINUOUS LEARNING STRATEGIES FOR AI

Staying current isn't a one-and-done project; it's an ongoing habit. Here are proven strategies to make learning both effective and sustainable:

1. **Structured Learning**

   Online Courses & Specializations: Platforms like Coursera, Udacity, and edX offer guided paths in machine learning, deep learning, and AI ethics. Set a schedule one module per week, for example and treat it like a work commitment.

   Certifications: If you work in regulated industries or large organizations, a recognized credential can validate your skills and open doors.

2. **Microlearning and Daily Practices**

   15-Minutes Deep Dives: Each day, spend a quarter hour reading a research summary, coding a small example, or watching a tutorial video.

   Flashcards for Theory: Use spaced repetition apps to memorize definitions, formulas, and key concepts (e.g., bias–variance trade-off, activation functions).

3. **Project-Based Mastery**

   Personal Sandbox: Maintain a GitHub repo of side projects chatbots, image classifiers, data visualizations where you apply new techniques immediately.

   Real-World Problems: Volunteer to build an AI solution for a nonprofit or community group. Real constraints sharpen your skills.

4. **Reflection and Documentation**

   Learning Journal: After each study session or project milestone, jot down what worked, what confused you, and next steps. Reviewing your notes reveals patterns in your growth.

   Blog or Newsletter: Teaching others via blog posts or short newsletters forces you to clarify your thinking and solidifies retention.

5. **Staying Agile with Playlists and Learning Paths**

   Curated Playlists: Assemble a playlist of foundational and advanced resources papers, videos, tutorials and update its quarterly.

   Learning "Sprints": Organize intensive, focused two-week sprints on specific topics (e.g., transformers, GANs), culminating in a small project or presentation.

6. **Balance Depth and Breadth**

   T-Shaped Learning: Aim for broad familiarity (the top bar of the T) across AI subfields NLP, computer vision, reinforcement learning while diving deep into one or two specialties (the vertical leg).

Staying Agile in a Changing Landscape

The ability to adapt is one of the most valuable skills in the AI era. Instead of trying to master every new tool or trend, focus on building a flexible mindset. Be open to change, willing to experiment, and ready to learn continuously. Curating your own learning resources such as playlists, reading lists, or project ideas helps you stay organized and focused. Periodically updating these resources ensures that your learning remains relevant.

Short learning sprints can also be effective. Focusing intensively on a specific topic for a limited time allows you to make rapid progress and build confidence.

Over time, these habits create a strong foundation that enables you to navigate change with ease.

CONCLUSION

Artificial Intelligence will continue to evolve and so should you.

In this chapter, you learned how to:

- Stay informed without feeling overwhelmed
- Evaluate new tools with clarity and confidence
- Build a strong network of peers and mentors
- Develop consistent and effective learning habits
- Adapt to change with a flexible mindset

The most important takeaway is this: **You do not need to know everything you need to keep learning.**

By building the right habits and staying curious, you can remain confident and capable in an ever-changing field.

The journey of learning AI does not end here. In fact, it is just beginning.

CHAPTER 21
NO-CODE AI TOOLS

INTRODUCTION

Imagine building your own application, automating repetitive tasks, or even creating intelligent systems without writing a single line of code. Not long ago, this would have required years of programming experience. Today, thanks to **No-Code AI tools**, it is accessible to anyone willing to learn and experiment.

No-Code platforms remove the technical barriers that once limited innovation. Instead of focusing on programming languages, you can now use visual interfaces, drag-and-drop builders, and pre-built components to bring your ideas to life.

When combined with Artificial Intelligence, these tools go beyond automation. They enable you to build systems that can analyze, generate, and respond intelligently.

In this chapter, you will not only understand the fundamentals of No-Code AI but also learn how to apply it in real-world scenarios. From exploring tools to building workflows and deploying applications, this chapter is designed to give you practical, hands-on value.

WHAT IS NO-CODE?

No-Code refers to tools and platforms that allow you to build applications, automate workflows, and manage data **without writing a single line of code.**

In traditional software development, creating even a simple application required programming knowledge. Today, No-Code tools remove that barrier by providing **visual interfaces, drag-and-drop builders, and pre-built components.**

In simple terms: No-Code means *building technology solutions using visual tools instead of programming languages*. You focus on *what to build*, not *how to code it.*

This shift empowers individuals to move from idea to execution faster than ever before.

WHY NO-CODE AI MATTERS

No-Code tools are changing the way individuals and businesses operate. They make technology accessible to everyone, regardless of technical background.

No-Code AI is transforming how individuals and organizations approach technology. It is not just about convenience it is about unlocking new possibilities.

1. **No Technical Skills Required:** Anyone can start using No-Code tools. You do not need to learn programming languages such as Python or JavaScript, making AI accessible to a much wider audience.
2. **Saves Time:** Tasks that once required days or weeks of development can now be completed in minutes or hours. This allows for faster execution and rapid experimentation.
3. **Cost-Effective:** Businesses can reduce dependency on developers for simple tools and automation, saving both time and financial resources.
4. **Faster Innovation:** Ideas can be tested quickly through prototypes and iterations, enabling faster learning and improvement.
5. **Empowers Individuals:** Students, professionals, and entrepreneurs can independently build

solutions, automate workflows, and solve real-world problems.

VIBE CODING: A MODERN APPROACH TO BUILDING WITH AI

What is vibe coding?

Vibe coding is a way of building app or software by **describing what you want in plain language**

and letting an AI write the code for you. Instead of typing out every line yourself, you have a conversation with an AI tool you tell it what to build, review what it generates, and refine through back-and-forth prompts until it works. This approach enables you to focus more on *what* you want to create rather than *how* to write every technical detail.

In essence, vibe coding transforms programming into a more **creative and accessible experience**, especially for beginners.

The term was invented by AI researcher Andrej Karpathy in early 2025. His framing: "fully give in to the vibes, embrace exponentials, and forget that the code even exists.

How it works in practice

- **Prompt:** You describe what you want: "Build a dashboard showing monthly revenue by product line."

- **Generate:** The AI produces working code (frontend, backend, database queries, etc.).
- **Review:** You check if the output matches your intent.
- **Iterate:** You refine through conversation: "Move the date filter to the top. Add a comparison to last quarter."

Tools That Enable Vibe Coding

Several modern AI-powered tools support this approach. Some of the most widely used include:

- ChatGPT
- GitHub Copilot
- Cursor IDE
- Replit

These tools act as intelligent assistants, helping you generate, refine, and understand code efficiently. It's especially powerful for people with domain expertise (finance, operations, customer success) who know *what* they need but don't know how to code it.

Why Vibe Coding Matters

Vibe coding is not just a trend; it represents a meaningful evolution in how people interact with technology. Its advantages are particularly impactful for beginners:

- **Faster Prototyping:** You can quickly turn ideas into working applications without extensive coding knowledge.
- **Experiential Learning:** By reviewing and modifying AI-generated code, you learn programming concepts in a practical and engaging way.
- **Idea Exploration:** It allows you to experiment freely, test concepts, and iterate rapidly.
- **Enhanced Productivity:** Even experienced developers use this approach to accelerate development and reduce repetitive tasks.

A Practical Example: Building a Simple Task Manager

To better understand vibe coding, consider a real-world scenario.

Imagine you want to build a simple "Daily Task Manager" application.

1. **Step 1: Define Your Intent**

   You begin by describing your requirement by using the below prompt either in ChatGPT or VS Code or Zapier Chat window:

   "Create a simple web application using HTML, CSS, and JavaScript that allows users to add, delete, and mark tasks as complete."

2. **Step 2: Generate the Initial Code**

   Using tools such as ChatGPT or GitHub Copilot, you receive a functional starting point that includes:

   - A structured layout (HTML)
   - Visual styling (CSS)
   - Interactive functionality (JavaScript)

3. **Step 3: Refine Through Iteration**

   This is where the "vibe" truly comes into play. You enhance your application by giving additional instructions:

   - "Add a dark mode feature"
   - "Store tasks using local storage"
   - "Improve the design for mobile devices"
   - "Include a progress indicator"

   With each prompt, the application evolves—guided by your vision.

4. **Step 4: Achieve a Working Solution**

   Within a short time, you have a fully functional application that:

   - Allows task creation and deletion
   - Tracks completion status
   - Saves data for future use

Vibe coding lowers the barrier to entry for software development and empowers individuals to bring their ideas to life more easily than ever before without writing every line of code manually.

For beginners, it offers a unique opportunity to **learn, build, and innovate simultaneously**.

LEADING NO-CODE AI TOOLS

Below are some of the most widely used No-Code tools that beginners can start with immediately.

1. Zapier

Zapier is often the first step for beginners. It allows you to connect applications and automate tasks with ease. For example, you can automatically save email attachments, send notifications, or update spreadsheets. Its simplicity makes it ideal for quick wins.

Key Features

- Connects thousands of applications
- Automates repetitive tasks
- Easy-to-use workflow builder

What You Can Do

- Save email attachments automatically to cloud storage
- Send notifications when a form is submitted

- Automate social media posting

Example Workflow

When a new email is received → Save attachment to cloud storage → Send notification

2. Make (formerly Integromat)

Make offers a more advanced experience. It provides a visual workflow builder where you can design complex processes with multiple steps, conditions, and logic. It is perfect for users who want greater control and more flexibility over their automation.

Key Features

- Visual workflow builder
- Multi-step automation
- Advanced logic and conditions

What You Can Do

- Create complex automation pipelines
- Integrate multiple apps in one workflow
- Customize processes with logic and filters

3. Notion

Notion acts as a central hub for organizing information. It combines note-taking, task management, and databases in one place. When paired with AI, it becomes a powerful tool for managing knowledge and productivity.

Key Features

- Notes and documentation
- Task and project management
- Built-in databases
- Custom dashboards

What You Can Do

- Organize personal or professional work
- Track goals and tasks
- Build knowledge bases

4. Airtable

Airtable brings together the simplicity of spreadsheets and the power of databases. It allows you to build structured systems for managing projects, tracking data, and even creating lightweight applications.

Key Features

- Spreadsheet-style interface
- Database capabilities
- Multiple views (grid, calendar, kanban)
- Built-in automation

What You Can Do

- Manage projects and workflows
- Track inventory or content
- Build lightweight applications

5. N8N

n8n takes flexibility to the next level. As an open-source platform, it allows you to create advanced workflows, integrate multiple systems, and even incorporate AI agents. It is especially useful for users who want more customization and control.

Key Features

- Visual workflow builder
- Multi-step automation
- Advanced logic and conditions

What You Can Do

- Automate Repetitive Tasks
- Integrate multiple apps in one workflow
- Customize processes with logic and filters

Best For

Users who want more flexibility and control compared to simpler tools.

Workflow Automation: Connects diverse tools like Slack, Google Sheets, Jira, and GitHub, allowing them to share data automatically.

AI Agent Integration: Builds sophisticated workflows with AI agents that can make decisions, process data, and execute tasks using prompt-based reasoning.

Data Transformation & Handling: Processes JSON, XML, and other data structures, enabling complex backend workflows that traditional "no-code" tools can't manage.

Self-Hosted Control: Because it is open-source, users can host n8n on their own infrastructure, ensuring data privacy and reducing reliance on third-party SaaS platforms.

Marketing & Sales Automation: Generates blog post drafts, manages CRM updates, and handles customer communication (e.g., sending messages via Line Chat).

Prototyping & Technical Workflows: Allows developers to use JavaScript to create complex, multi-step logic without building custom integration scripts from scratch

How No-Code and AI Work Together

Individually, no-code tools automate tasks. AI tools generate insights and content. When combined, they create something far more powerful intelligent automation.

Imagine a simple scenario.

A user fills out a form on your website. That information is instantly processed by an AI system, which generates a personalized response. The system then sends an email, updates a database, and notifies your team all automatically.

This is not just automation. It is a system that can understand, decide, and act. This combination allows you to build workflows that respond dynamically to real-world situations, making your processes smarter and more efficient.

Sample Workflow

A user submits a form → AI generates a response → The response is automatically emailed to the user

This combination allows anyone to build **smart, automated systems without coding.**

Why Automation with AI Matters

In today's fast-paced world, repetitive work slows down productivity. AI automation helps individuals and businesses:

- Save time by eliminating manual tasks
- Improve accuracy and consistency

- Scale operations without increasing workload
- Focus on creative and strategic work

Key Components of AI Automation

Before building workflows, it's important to understand the basic building blocks:

1. **Trigger:** This is the event that initiates the process or starting point of automation, such as receiving an email or submitting a form.
2. **Action:** Once triggered, an action takes place. This might involve collecting data, storing information, save the email data or sending it to another tool.
3. **AI Processing:** This is where the system analyzes data, generates content, generate a reply or summary or makes decisions.
4. **Output:** The workflow produces an output or final result. This could be sending a response, updating a system, or triggering another action.

Example: Send an automated email response

By combining these elements, you can design workflows that are both automated and intelligent.

DIFFERENT WORKFLOWS FOR NO-CODE AUTOMATION:

Workflow 1: AI-Powered Email Auto-Reply

Objective

Incoming emails can be analyzed and responded automatically using AI-generated replies. This saves time while maintaining professional communication.

Tools Needed

- Email platform (e.g., Gmail)
- Automation tool (e.g., Zapier or Make)
- AI tool (e.g., ChatGPT)

Step-by-Step Process

1. **Set Trigger:** When a new email is received
2. **Extract Content:** Capture subject and message body
3. **Send to AI:** Provide a prompt such as: "*Write a professional reply to this email: [email content]*"
4. **Generate Response:** AI creates a suitable reply
5. **Send Email Automatically:** The response is sent back to the sender

Workflow 2: Social Media Content Automation

Objective

In social media management, content ideas can be transformed into posts, formatted, and scheduled automatically. This ensures consistency without constant manual effort.

Tools Needed

- Content source (Google Sheets or Notion)
- Automation platform
- AI tool for content generation

Step-by-Step Process

1. **Trigger:** New entry added to content sheet
2. **AI Content Generation:** Prompt AI to create a post: *"Create a LinkedIn post based on this topic: [topic]"*
3. **Format Content:** Add hashtags and structure
4. **Publish or Schedule:** Automatically post or queue it

Workflow 3: Lead Management Automation

Objective

In lead management, customer inquiries can be captured, analyzed, and responded to instantly. This improves response time and enhances the customer experience.

Tools Needed

- Form tool (Google Forms)
- Airtable or CRM
- Automation tool
- AI tool

Step-by-Step Process

1. **Trigger:** A user submits a form
2. **Store Data:** Save details in a database
3. **AI Personalization:** Generate a customized response: *"Write a welcome email for a new customer interested in [service]"*
4. **Send Email:** Automatically deliver response

Workflow 4: AI Content Repurposing

Objective

Content repurposing is another powerful use case. Turn one piece of content into multiple formats. A single blog post can be converted into summaries, newsletters, and social media content, maximizing its value.

Example

Convert a blog into:

- Social media posts
- Email newsletter

- Short summary

Steps

- Input original content
- Ask AI to Summarize, Rewrite, Extract key points
- Save outputs in different platforms

Workflow 5: Daily Task Automation

Objective

Automate your daily planning and productivity. AI can prioritize tasks, create schedules, and deliver daily plans, helping you stay focused and organized.

Steps

1. Collect tasks from different sources
2. Use AI to prioritize task, create a schedule
3. Send daily plan to your email or workspace

Real-Life Example

Imagine you run a small business:

- A customer fills out a contact form
- AI generates a personalized reply
- The email is sent instantly
- Customer data is stored automatically

This entire process happens **without manual effort.**

BUILD APPS WITHOUT CODING: STEP-BY-STEP TUTORIAL

Follow these five stages to create a simple sentiment-analysis survey bot that classifies user feedback and responds appropriately.

1. **Define Your Objective**

   - **Problem:** Customers leave open-ended feedback; you want to triage sentiments automatically.
   - **Desired outcome:** Tag comments as positive, neutral, or negative and trigger follow-up messages.

   A clear objective guides data collection, model selection, and chatbot design.

2. **Prepare and Label Your Data**

   Collect a sample of feedback (150–200 entries per category). Organize data in a spreadsheet with two columns: "Text" and "Label."

   Ensure diversity: include slang, typos, and varied lengths.

   Upload to your chosen platform (e.g., Google AutoML Natural Language).

   Quality labels are the foundation of an accurate model. Review examples to avoid ambiguity.

3. **Train and Evaluate Your Model**

    Launch training with default settings—no technical adjustments needed.

    Monitor progress: training may take 10–20 minutes.

    Examine evaluation metrics:

    - **Accuracy:** overall correctness
    - Precision & recall for each label
    - Confusion matrix to spot misclassifications

    If "neutral" feedback misclassifies often, add more examples or refine label definitions. Iterate until performance meets your threshold (e.g., 85% accuracy).

4. **Design the Chatbot Interface**

    Select a no-code chatbot builder (e.g., IBM Watson Assistant or Power Virtual Agents).

    Create intents and entities relevant to feedback collection.

    Add a dialog node that calls your sentiment-analysis API.

    Map API responses to messages:

    - **Positive:** "Thank you! We're thrilled you enjoyed it."

- **Neutral:** "Thanks for your thoughts. How can we improve?"
- **Negative:** "We're sorry to hear that. A team member will reach out."

Drag buttons and input fields to guide users through the conversation, ensuring a smooth experience.

5. **Deploy and Monitor**

   Embed the chatbot on your website or integrate with messaging platforms like Slack.

   Run real-world tests by submitting sample feedback.

   Monitor logs, user satisfaction scores, and API usage dashboards.

   Tweak response messages or retrain the model with new data to improve accuracy.

   Within a few hours, you've created and launched a conversational AI assistant no coding required.

REAL-WORLD EXAMPLE: IMAGE CLASSIFICATION APP

A photography blogger wants to automatically tag uploaded photos by category (landscape, portrait, wildlife). Using a no-code computer-vision tool:

1. Collect and label 500 sample images in folders by category.

2. Upload and train an AutoML Vision model.
3. Review performance and adjust labels.
4. Integrate with a website using a prebuilt plugin.
5. Automatically tag new images and display category filters for visitors.

This automation saves hours of manual tagging each week and enhances the browsing experience.

OVERCOMING COMMON CHALLENGES

1. **Data Quality:** Data quality remains one of the most critical factors. Poor data leads to poor results, so it is important to invest time in cleaning and organizing your data.
2. **Platform Limitations:** Platform limitations may also arise. Some tools may not support advanced features. In such cases, combining multiple tools or using integrations can help. Combine no-code with lightweight scripts via built-in connectors or webhooks.
3. **Cost Controls:** Cost management is another consideration. As usage grows, costs can increase. Monitoring usage, set budget alerts, and leverage free quotas for development and setting limits ensures that your projects remain sustainable.
4. **Security and Compliance:** Security and compliance are equally important. Always ensure

that sensitive data is handled securely and that you follow best practices for privacy. Ensure data encryption, review vendor certifications (ISO, GDPR), and implement role-based access.

By addressing these challenges early, you can build more reliable and effective solutions.

SCALING YOUR NO-CODE AI PROJECTS

Once you are comfortable with basic workflows, the next step is scaling:

Workflow Automation: You can connect multiple workflows to create end-to-end systems that automate entire processes. For example, a business workflow can handle everything from data collection to reporting. (e.g., invoice processing, approval routing).

Analytics Dashboards: Integrating AI outputs into dashboards allows you to visualize insights and make informed decisions. Feed predictions into Business Intelligence tools like Power BI or Looker for real-time insights.

Cross-Platform Reach: Expanding across platforms ensures that your solutions reach users wherever they are whether on web, mobile, or messaging platforms. Deploy bots on web, mobile, and messaging apps to meet users wherever they are.

Collaborative Templates: Collaboration also plays a key role. Sharing workflows and templates with teams encourages innovation and consistency. Share project blueprints across your team or organization to foster an AI-driven culture.

Governance Framework: Implement version control, labeling standards, and audit trails to maintain quality and compliance.

CONCLUSION

No-code AI tools are redefining what is possible. They remove technical barriers, accelerate innovation, and empower individuals to build intelligent systems with ease.

In this chapter, you explored how to:

- Understand the fundamentals of no-code AI
- Use popular tools to build workflows
- Combine automation with intelligence
- Create real-world applications
- Overcome challenges and scale solutions

The most important takeaway is this: **You do not need technical expertise to create powerful AI solutions, you need curiosity, creativity, and the willingness to start.**

Begin with a simple idea. Experiment with a tool. Build your first workflow.

As you continue, you will discover that AI is not just a technology, it is a capability that anyone can harness.

And that includes you.

CHAPTER 22

GETTING STARTED WITH AI PROJECTS

INTRODUCTION

Starting your first AI project can feel intimidating. You may come across unfamiliar terms like machine learning, neural networks, and data pipelines. The tools might seem complex, and the process may appear overwhelming. But here's the truth:

Every AI expert you see today started exactly where you are now.

The most effective way to learn Artificial Intelligence is not by reading alone it is by building, experimenting, and learning through doing.

This chapter is designed to guide you step by step. You will explore practical beginner-friendly project ideas and learn a structured approach to building your own

AI solutions with confidence even if you have no prior experience.

By the end of this chapter, you will not only understand how AI projects are built but also feel ready to start your own journey.

SIMPLE PROJECT IDEAS

One of the best ways to begin is by working on small, focused projects. These projects help you understand core concepts while building real-world skills.

Rule-Based Chatbot

- **Description:** Develop a conversational chatbot capable of answering basic user queries using predefined if-then logic and keyword matching techniques
- **Why This Project is Valuable:** This project introduces the fundamentals of natural language interaction, including processing user input, identifying keywords, and generating appropriate responses without requiring advanced machine learning knowledge.
- **Tools:** Python, basic string processing or the Rasa framework.
- **Outcome:** A functional chatbot that can be integrated into a simple website or messaging platform.

Image Classifier with Transfer Learning

- **Description:** Create an image classification system using pre-trained neural network models such as MobileNet or ResNet to categorize images into predefined classes, such as cats versus dogs, fruit categories, or handwritten digits.
- **Why this Project is Valuable:** Transfer learning enables beginners to build powerful image-recognition applications without requiring massive datasets or expensive computing resources.
- **Tools:** TensorFlow/Keras or PyTorch, a small labeled dataset from sources like Kaggle or your own photo collection.
- **Outcome:** A working image-recognition application that can be executed locally or deployed as a web service.

Sentiment Analysis on Social Media Post.

- **Description:** Build a sentiment analysis model that evaluates social media posts or tweets related to a specific topic and classifies them as positive, negative, or neutral.
- **Why this Project is Valuable:** This project helps learners understand essential natural language processing (NLP) tasks such as text

cleaning, feature extraction, and classification techniques.

- **Tools:** Python, NLTK for preprocessing, scikit-learn for models.
- **Outcome:** A dashboard or report that visualizes sentiment trends over time.

Recommendation Engine

- **Description:** Design a recommendation system that suggests books, movies, products, or other content based on user preferences and historical behavior.
- **Why This Project is Valuable:** This project introduces recommendation algorithms such as collaborative filtering and content-based filtering, which are widely used in modern digital platforms.
- **Tools:** Python, pandas for data handling, surprise or lightFM libraries for recommendations.
- **Outcome:** A simple web page or interfaces that provides personalized recommendations to users.

Data Visualization Dashboard

- **Description:** Create an interactive dashboard that collects and visualizes real-world datasets, such as stock market prices, public health statistics, or weather information.

- **Why it Valuable:** This project teaches essential skills in data collection, API integration, data processing, and visual storytelling, all of which are highly valuable in applied AI and analytics.
- **Tools:** Jupyter, pandas, Plotly Dash or Streamlit.
- **Outcome:** A shareable dashboard that updates dynamically and enables users to explore trends interactively.6. Text Summarization Tool.

Text Summarization Tool

- **Description:** Develop a text summarization application that extracts key sentences from long articles, reports, or documents to generate concise summaries.
- **Why it works:** This project provides practical exposure to natural language processing workflows, including tokenization, sentence scoring, and summary generation.
- **Tools:** Python, NLTK or Hugging Face Transformers for more advanced models.

- **Outcome:** A command-line tool or web application capable of converting lengthy content into concise and readable summaries.

DEVELOPING A STEP-BY-STEP MINDSET FOR AI PROJECTS

Building AI projects successfully requires more than just tools it requires a structured mindset. Following a clear process will help you stay organized, reduce frustration, and make consistent progress.

Clearly Define the Problem

- Identify the business challenge or personal objective you want to solve.
- Create a concise problem statement, such as: "I want to classify emails as spam or non-spam."
- Determine measurable success metrics, including accuracy, precision, recall, or user engagement.

Gather and Understand the Data

- Collect datasets relevant to the problem from public sources such as Kaggle, the UCI Machine Learning Repository, or open APIs.
- Analyze the data to identify missing values, biases, and overall distribution patterns.

- Clean and preprocess the dataset by handling null values, standardizing formats, and preparing labels if necessary.

Select Appropriate Tools and Frameworks

- Begin with beginner-friendly libraries such as scikit-learn or Keras before exploring lower-level frameworks.
- Use tutorials, sample notebooks, and community resources as references.
- Maintain a clean development environment using virtual environments or containerization tools such as Docker.

Build a Simple Baseline Model

- Start with a straightforward approach, such as rule-based logic or logistic regression.
- Evaluate the model's initial performance to establish a baseline benchmark.
- Recognize and appreciate incremental progress, even if the initial accuracy is modest.

Iterate and Improve Continuously

- Analyze model errors and identify areas where predictions are inaccurate.

- Experiment with feature engineering, advanced algorithms, and hyperparameter tuning techniques.
- Track experiments systematically using version control systems or tools such as MLflow.

Document and Share Your Work

- Create clear README documentation and properly comment your code.
- Publish projects on platforms such as GitHub to showcase your work and receive feedback from the community.
- Sharing knowledge and explaining concepts to others strengthens both technical understanding and professional credibility.

Reflect and Plan Future Enhancements

- Evaluate the lessons learned throughout the project lifecycle.
- Identify challenges encountered and document how they were resolved.
- Consider future improvements, such as integrating additional datasets, enhancing the user experience, or implementing more advanced AI techniques.

CONCLUSION

Starting an AI project does not require advanced academic qualifications or significant financial investment. What truly matters is curiosity, consistency, and a willingness to learn through experimentation. By working on small, practical projects and following a structured approach, you can gradually transform your understanding of AI from theory into real-world applications. Each project you build strengthens your confidence, sharpens your skills, and prepares you for more advanced challenges.

The most important thing to remember is this: **You do not need to know everything before you start, you just need to start.**

Your journey into AI begins with a single project. And with every step you take, new opportunities for learning, innovation, and growth will open up.

The future of AI is not just for experts; it is for creators like you.

CHAPTER 23

PRACTICAL AI USE CASES

Everyday Productivity

- Draft emails in seconds using ChatGPT
- Summarize long articles or PDFs
- Turn rough notes into polished documents
- Create daily to-do lists from messy thoughts
- Rewrite messages in a professional tone
- Generate meeting agendas
- Convert bullet points into full reports
- Brainstorm ideas for any topic
- Translate text between languages
- Create quick how-to guides for tasks

Work & Office Productivity

- Write weekly status reports (great for PMs)
- Generate PowerPoint outlines from a topic
- Draft SOPs and documentation
- Convert meeting notes into action items
- Create job descriptions
- Analyze spreadsheets (summaries, trends)
- Prepare interview questions
- Write performance reviews
- Automate repetitive workflows with n8n
- Draft business proposals

Communication & Writing

- Write cold emails and follow-ups
- Generate LinkedIn posts
- Create blog articles
- Improve grammar and clarity
- Write customer support replies
- Draft apology or escalation emails
- Create newsletters
- Generate storytelling content
- Turn ideas into scripts (YouTube, reels)
- Rewrite content for different audiences

Business & Entrepreneurship

- Generate business ideas
- Create business plans
- Conduct basic market research
- Write product descriptions
- Generate ad copy
- Analyze competitors
- Create pricing strategies
- Build FAQs for customers
- Draft contracts (first version)
- Generate pitch decks

Marketing & Content Creation

- Create social media calendars
- Generate Instagram captions
- Design visuals with Canva AI tools
- Create AI-generated images using Midjourney
- Write SEO-friendly blog posts
- Generate keywords for content
- Create video scripts
- Repurpose content across platforms
- Generate ad headlines
- Analyze audience personas

Tech & Development

- Generate code snippets with GitHub Copilot
- Debug code faster
- Convert code between languages
- Write API documentation
- Generate test cases
- Build simple apps using no-code AI tools
- Automate scripts
- Learn new programming concepts quickly

Learning & Education

- Explain complex topics simply
- Create study notes
- Generate quizzes and flashcards
- Summarize textbooks
- Create learning roadmaps
- Practice interview questions
- Learn new skills faster
- Get step-by-step explanations
- Create mind maps
- Simulate a tutor for any subject

Personal Life & Daily Use

- Plan travel itineraries
- Create workout plans
- Generate meal plans
- Manage personal finances (basic planning)
- Write resumes and cover letters
- Prepare for interviews
- Draft personal messages
- Plan events
- Get book or movie recommendations
- Solve everyday problems creatively

Advanced (But Still Beginner-Friendly)

- Build AI chatbots for websites
- Automate email workflows
- Create AI-powered dashboards
- Generate voiceovers
- Transcribe audio to text
- Analyze customer feedback
- Create internal knowledge assistants
- Build simple AI tools without coding

GLOSSARY OF AI TERMINOLOGIES

(Essential Definitions Every AI Practitioner Must Know)

A

Agent (AI Agent) An AI system that can autonomously plan, decide, and take actions to complete complex multi-step tasks without constant human guidance.

Algorithm A set of rules or instructions that a computer follows to solve a problem or make a decision.

Artificial General Intelligence (AGI) A hypothetical form of AI that can perform any intellectual task that a human can do, across all domains.

Artificial Intelligence (AI) The simulation of human intelligence by machines, enabling them to learn, reason, problem-solve, and make decisions.

Artificial Neural Network (ANN) A computing system inspired by the human brain, consisting of interconnected nodes that process and learn from data.

Autoregressive Model A model that generates output one element at a time, with each element informed by all previously generated elements.

B

Backpropagation A training technique where a neural network adjusts its internal weights by working backwards from errors to improve future predictions.

Bias (AI Bias) Systematic errors in AI outputs caused by flawed assumptions, unrepresentative training data, or prejudiced human input.

Big Data Extremely large datasets that traditional software cannot process, often used to train AI models.

C

Chatbot A software application designed to simulate human conversation, powered by rules or AI language models.

Claude Anthropic's AI assistant, built with a strong focus on safety, honesty, and helpfulness, known for long-context reasoning and nuanced analysis.

Classification An AI task where the model assigns input data into predefined categories or labels.

Clustering An unsupervised learning technique that groups similar data points together without predefined labels.

Computer Vision A field of AI that enables machines to interpret and understand visual information from images and videos.

Context Window The maximum amount of text an AI model can process and remember at one time during a conversation.

Convolutional Neural Network (CNN) A type of neural network specialized for processing visual data like images and videos.

D

DALL·E OpenAI's AI image generation model that creates images from text descriptions.

Data Augmentation A technique to artificially expand training datasets by creating modified versions of existing data.

Deep Learning A subset of machine learning using multi-layered neural networks to learn complex patterns from large amounts of data.

Diffusion Model A generative AI model that creates images by gradually refining random noise into coherent visuals.

E

Embedding A numerical representation of words, sentences, or concepts that captures their meaning in a format AI can process.

Emergent Behavior Unexpected capabilities that arise in large AI models that were not explicitly programmed or anticipated.

Epoch One complete pass through the entire training dataset during the AI model training process.

F

Few-Shot Learning Teaching an AI to perform a task by providing only a small number of examples within the prompt.

Fine-Tuning Further training a pre-trained AI model on a specific dataset to specialize it for a particular task.

Foundation Model A large AI model trained on broad data that can be adapted to a wide range of downstream tasks.

G

Gemini Google DeepMind's multimodal AI model capable of understanding and generating text, images, audio, and video.

Generative AI systems that can create new content (text, images, audio, video, or code) based on patterns learned from training data.

GPT (Generative Pre-trained Transformer) OpenAI's family of large language models, including ChatGPT, known for generating human-like text across diverse tasks.

GPU (Graphics Processing Unit) Specialized hardware originally designed for graphics but now widely used to accelerate AI model training.

H

Hallucination When an AI model generates information that sounds plausible but is factually incorrect or completely fabricated.

Hyperparameter A configuration setting that controls how an AI model is trained, such as learning rate or number of layers.

I

Inference The process of using a trained AI model to generate predictions or outputs from new input data.

Instruction Tuning A fine-tuning technique where models are trained to follow natural language instructions more accurately.

L

Large Language Model (LLM) A type of AI model trained on massive text datasets, capable of understanding and generating human language at scale.

Latency The time delay between submitting a prompt to an AI model and receiving its response.

Learning Rate A hyperparameter that controls how quickly or slowly an AI model updates its weights during training.

M

Machine Learning (ML) A subset of AI where systems learn from data and improve their performance over time without being explicitly programmed.

Model A mathematical representation trained on data that an AI system uses to make predictions or generate outputs.

Multimodal AI An AI system capable of processing and generating multiple types of data, such as text, images, audio, and video simultaneously.

N

Natural Language Processing (NLP) A branch of AI focused on enabling machines to understand, interpret, and generate human language.

Natural Language Generation (NLG) The AI capability to produce coherent and contextually appropriate human language from structured data.

Neural Network A computational model inspired by the human brain, consisting of layers of interconnected nodes that process data.

O

Overfitting When an AI model learns training data too well, including its noise and errors, causing poor performance on new data.

OpenAI The AI research company behind GPT, ChatGPT, DALL·E, and other influential AI systems.

P

Parameters The internal variables of an AI model that are adjusted during training to improve its performance and accuracy.

Prompt The input text or instruction given to an AI model to guide its response or output.

Prompt Engineering The skill of designing and refining prompts to get the most accurate, relevant, and useful outputs from AI models.

Pre-training The initial phase of training a large AI model on a broad dataset before fine-tuning for specific tasks.

R

RAG (Retrieval-Augmented Generation) A technique that enhances AI responses by retrieving relevant external information before generating an answer.

Reasoning An AI model's ability to analyze information, draw logical conclusions, and solve multi-step problems.

Reinforcement Learning A machine learning approach where an AI learns by receiving rewards or penalties based on its actions.

RLHF (Reinforcement Learning from Human Feedback) A training technique where human evaluators rate AI outputs to help the model learn preferred behaviors.

S

Supervised Learning A machine learning approach where models are trained on labeled data with known correct answers.

System Prompt Hidden instructions given to an AI model before a conversation begins, shaping its behavior and persona.

T

Temperature A parameter that controls the randomness of AI outputs — lower values produce more predictable responses, higher values more creative ones.

Token The basic unit of text that AI models process — roughly a word or part of a word.

Transformer The revolutionary neural network architecture introduced in 2017 that powers most modern large language models.

Transfer Learning Using knowledge gained from training on one task to improve performance on a different but related task.

Turing Test A test proposed by Alan Turing to evaluate whether a machine can exhibit intelligent behavior indistinguishable from a human.

U

Underfitting When an AI model is too simple to capture patterns in the data, resulting in poor performance on both training and new data.

Unsupervised Learning A machine learning approach where models find hidden patterns in data without labeled examples.

V

Vector Database A specialized database that stores data as numerical vectors, enabling fast similarity searches used in RAG systems.

Z

Zero-Shot Learning The ability of an AI model to perform a task it has never explicitly been trained on, based solely on instructions.

RECOMMENDED RESOURCES & TOOLS

AI ASSISTANTS & PLATFORMS

Tool	Company	Best For	Website
ChatGPT	OpenAI	Writing, coding, creativity	chat.openai.com
Claude	Anthropic	Analysis, reasoning, long documents	claude.ai
Gemini	Google	Research, productivity, multimodal tasks	gemini.google.com
Copilot	Microsoft	Office productivity, search	copilot.microsoft.com
Meta AI	Meta	Social, everyday tasks	meta.ai

AI IMAGE & VIDEO GENERATION

Tool	Best For
DALL·E 3	Text-to-image via ChatGPT

Tool	Best For
Midjourney	High-quality artistic image generation
Stable Diffusion	Open-source image generation
Runway ML	AI video generation and editing
Adobe Firefly	Creative professionals using Adobe suite
Sora	OpenAI's text-to-video generation
Nano Banana	High Quality Image and Photo

AI CODING TOOLS

Tool	Best For
GitHub Copilot	In-editor AI code completion
Claude Code	Agentic coding and codebase navigation
Cursor	AI-powered code editor
Replit AI	Beginner-friendly AI coding environment
Tabnine	AI code completion across IDEs

AI PRODUCTIVITY TOOLS

Tool	Best For
Notion AI	Notes, documents, and project management
Grammarly	AI writing and grammar assistance
Otter.ai	AI meeting transcription
Perplexity AI	AI-powered research and search
Beautiful.ai	AI-powered presentation creation

AI LEARNING PLATFORMS

Platform	Best For
Coursera	Structured AI and ML courses
DeepLearning.AI	Andrew Ng's world-class AI courses
Fast.ai	Practical deep learning for coders
Google AI	Free Google AI learning resources
Anthropic Academy	Learning to use Claude effectively

REFERENCES & FURTHER READING

Beginner-Friendly Online Courses

- Coursera-AI for Everyone by Andrew Ng A non-technical introduction to AI concepts, ideal for beginners.
- edX-Introduction to Artificial Intelligence Covers foundational AI topics from leading universities.
- Udemy-Practical AI & Machine Learning Courses Offers hands-on learning with real-world examples.

Foundational Books on AI

- Artificial Intelligence: A Modern Approach by Stuart Russell and Peter Norvig A comprehensive introduction to the core concepts of AI, widely used in academic and professional settings.

- Life 3.0: Being Human in the Age of Artificial Intelligence by Max Tegmark Explores the future impact of AI on society, ethics, and human life.
- Machine Learning Yearning by Andrew Ng A practical guide to building machine learning systems, especially useful for beginners transitioning into applied AI.

AI Tools and Platforms

- **OpenAI:** Provides tools like ChatGPT for learning and experimentation.
- **Google Gemini:** Offers multimodal AI capabilities and integration with productivity tools.
- **Anthropic Claude:** Focuses on safe and reliable AI systems.
- **Hugging Face:** Provides open-source models, datasets, and tools for NLP and AI development.

Communities and Learning Platforms

- **Kaggle:** A platform for datasets, competitions, and hands-on AI practice.

- **Stack Overflow:** A valuable resource for troubleshooting and technical discussions.
- **GitHub:** Explore open-source AI projects and collaborate with developers worldwide.

Newsletters and Staying Updated

- **The Batch by Andrew Ng:** Weekly updates on AI trends and insights.
- **MIT Technology Review:** Covers the latest advancements in AI and emerging technologies.
- **Towards Data Science:** Practical articles and tutorials on AI, data science, and machine learning.

ACKNOWLEDGEMENTS

Writing *AI for Beginners 2026* has been a meaningful and rewarding journey and like all meaningful journeys, it was not completed alone.

I would like to express my sincere gratitude to the researchers, engineers, and visionaries at organizations such as OpenAI, Anthropic, Microsoft and Google DeepMind. Their groundbreaking work in Artificial Intelligence has not only inspired this book but has also shaped the future of technology in ways that make learning and innovation accessible to all.

My heartfelt thanks go to my colleagues, mentors, and senior leaders who continuously encouraged me to explore, learn, and share knowledge. Your guidance and support played an important role in shaping both my thinking and this book.

I am deeply grateful to the early readers and reviewers whose honest feedback helped refine every chapter. Your insights, suggestions, and thoughtful critiques have significantly improved the clarity and value of this book.

I would also like to acknowledge the global AI community, the researchers publishing open papers, the developers building open-source tools, the educators creating accessible learning resources, and the communities that share knowledge freely. Your collective efforts are the foundation that makes AI accessible to everyone, not just a select few.

To my editor and publishing support, thank you for your belief in this work, your patience in refining it, and your dedication in helping bring this book to life for readers around the world.

To every reader who picks up this book, whether you are a beginner taking your first step or a professional expanding your knowledge, this book is written for you. Your curiosity, willingness to learn, and commitment to growth are what will ensure that Artificial Intelligence continues to serve humanity in meaningful and responsible ways.

Finally, I would like to thank my family and friends. Your patience, encouragement, and unwavering support during long hours of writing, review, optimization and reflection made this journey possible. This book is as much yours as it is mine.

This work is dedicated to anyone who has ever felt left behind by technology and chose to move forward anyway.

www.ingramcontent.com/pod-product-compliance
Lightning Source LLC
LaVergne TN
LVHW100255210926
848480LV00003B/924